The People of
SOUTH WEST SCOTLAND
at Home and Abroad
1800 - 1850

By
David Dobson

CLEARFIELD

Copyright © 2022
by David Dobson
All Rights Reserved

Published for Clearfield Company by
Genealogical Publishing Company
Baltimore, Maryland
2022

ISBN: 9780806359465

INTRODUCTION

The People of South West Scotland, at Home and Abroad, 1800-1850 identifies people in or from the neighbouring counties of Renfrewshire, Ayrshire, Dumfries-shire, Kirkcudbrightshire, and Wigtownshire, between 1800 and 1850. [NB. The last three counties have since been formed into the administrative unit of 'Dumfries and Galloway'.] South West Scotland originally contained about 150 parishes, some of which subsequently merged. The main burghs were Renfrew, Greenock, Largs, Kilmarnock, Paisley, Ardrossan, Troon, Ayr, Stranraer, Wigtown, Kirkcudbright, Sanquhar, Dumfries, and Annan. The regional economy was based on farming, fishing, mining, iron and steel manufacture, engineering, textiles, and it possessed trading links especially with Ireland and North America. Emigration from South West Scotland to Ulster was substantial in the seventeenth century, but by the nineteenth century the destination shifted increasingly to North America and Australasia.

The information in this book is derived from a wide range of sources such as court records, contemporary newspapers and journals, monumental inscriptions, and documents found in archives. The entries bring together emigrants, their origins, and destinations--especially in North America, the West Indies, and Australasia – with their kin who remained in Scotland.

A crucial source for this era of Scottish history and genealogy is the Statistical Account of Scotland [the O.S.A] established by Sir John Sinclair. The O.S.A. is a collection of reports by nearly one thousand parish ministers in Scotland compiled between 1791 and 1799. These reports cover a wide range of topics for each parish, including geography, education, history, agriculture, shipping, population, and religious denominations. It is therefore a unique source of useful background for the family historian as it provides an insight into Scottish society at the end of the eighteenth century.

The rapid changes in Scottish society in the early 1800s ultimately resulted in the New Statistical Account being researched between 1832 and 1845. Both it and the O.S.A. were published and copies may be found in most of the older libraries in Scotland; however, they are both available on the website of the National Library of Scotland.

David Dobson
Dundee, Scotland, 2022

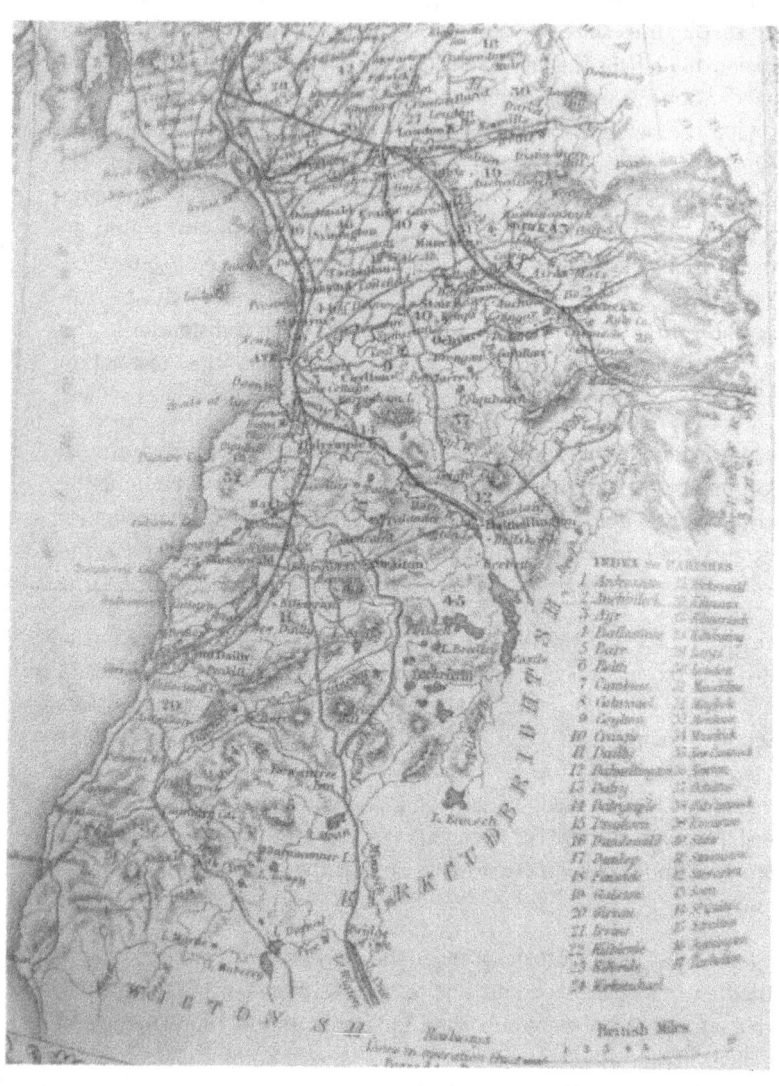

Ayrshire, with parishes

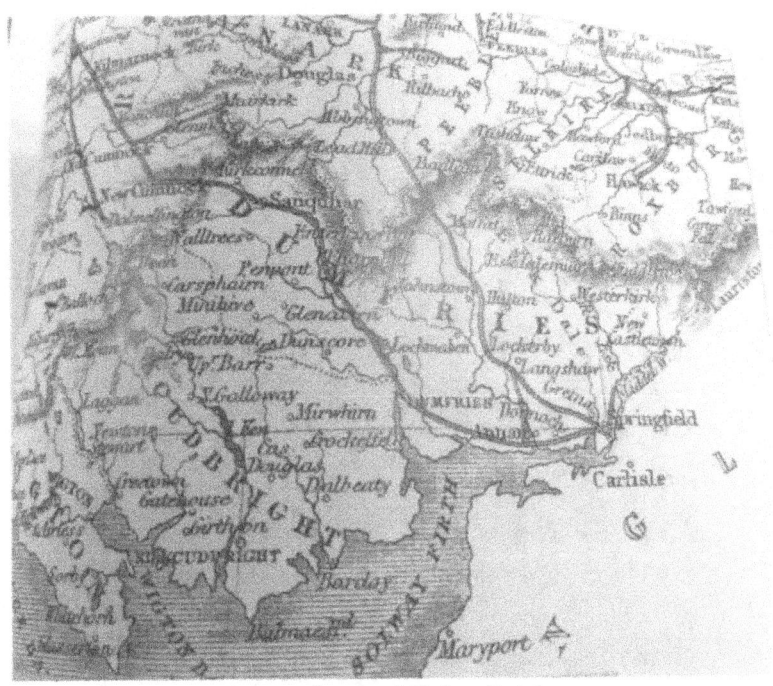

Dumfries and Kirkcudbright

Stranraer, Dumfries and Galloway

Ayr, from Brown Carrick

The Fish Cross, Ayr

Ayr, circa 1820

THE PEOPLE OF SOUTH WEST SCOTLAND,
AT HOME AND ABROAD, 1800-1850.

ADAIR, ISOBEL, in Ayr, testament, 1798, Comm. Glasgow. [NRS]

ADAIR, Dr JAMES M., in Newton Ayr, probate 7 December 1801. [Probate 11.1366.153, TNA]

ADAIR, JOHN, born 3 July 1824 in Portpatrick, Wigtownshire, emigrated on the Collingwood to Quebec in 1848, settled in New York in 1850, died in New York in 1850, died in Newark, New Jersey, on 10 November 1912. [ANY]

ADAM, ROBERT, born 9 December 1760 in West Kilbride, son of Reverend John Adam and his wife Elizabeth Parker, a merchant in Fayetteville, North Carolina, died in 1804. [F.3.202]

ADAM, THOMAS, from Johnstone, Renfrewshire, a divinity student in 1823, a surgeon in Barrhead, Renfrewshire, emigrated to America. [AUPC]

AFFLECK, CHARLES, was found guilty of forgery at Ayr in 1815 and was sentenced to transportation to the colonies for 14 years. [NRS.GD1.959]

AFFLECK, JAMES, a minister in Middelburg, Holland, then in London, later in Dumfries, testament, 1800, Dumfries, 1800. [NRS]

AGNEW, JOHN, master of the Caledonia of Stranraer trading between Glasgow and Ayr in 1818. [NRS.E504.4.14]

AIKEN, ANDREW, a staymaker in Kilmarnock, a petition, 1802. [NRS.CS97.1014]

AIKEN, JOHN, son of John Aiken at the Bridge of Johnstone, Renfrewshire, a wright Fayetteville, North Carolion Carncarron Estate in Jamaica, 1799. [NRS.CS18.712.13

AINSLEY, HEW, born in Bargeny Mains, Ayrshire, emigrated to America in 1822, an author who died in Louisville, Kentucky, in 1878. [SSA]

AIRD, JAMES, from Ayrshire, a fur trader in Canada, died at Prairie du Chien on 27 February 1819. [DCB]

AITCHISON, REBECCA, born in 1780s, daughter of Thomas Aitchison in Kellwood, Caerlaverock, Dumfries-shire, married ....Dobie a farmer, settled in Binghamton, Broome County, New York, died there in December 1857. [DGH.5.2.1858]

AITKEN, HUGH, second son of John Aitken in Ayr, died in Quebec on 1 November 1839. [SG.827]

AITKEN, ROBERT, born 1801, a weaver in Paisley, imprisoned in Glasgow accused of theft in 1820. [NRS.AD14.20.19]

ALEXANDER, F., emigrated from Kirkcudbrightshire to New York in June 1850, died in Alabama on 20 September 1850. [DGH.3.10.1850]

ALEXANDER, GEORGE, born 4 August 1828, graduated MA from Glasgow University in 1853, a United Presbyterian minister at Ebenezer, Jamaica, died in Glasgow on 15 March 1895. [GG.10]

ALEXANDER, HECTOR, in Dumfries, Prince William County, Virginia, brother of John Alexander of Mountpleasant, then in Greenock, a sasine, 1824. [NRS.RS54.1985]

ALEXANDER, ISOBEL, daughter of Patrick Alexander of Crossclays, testament, 1798, Comm. Glasgow. [NRS]

ALEXANDER, JOHN, a merchant in Greenock, Renfrewshire, and his wife Jean R. Copeland, parents of James Alexander, born 1854, who died in Auckland, New Zealand, on 25 May 1879, also, of William C. Alexander, born 1854, died in Wellington, N.Z., on 23 May 1907, and Thomas Alexander, born 1870, died in Pahi, N.Z., on 28 September 1889. [Inverkip gravestone, Renfrewshire]

ALEXANDER, MARGARET, born 1791, daughter of John Shaw Alexander of Mackilston, married John Johnston, died in Geneva, Ontario County, New York, on 30 August 1854. [Dalry gravestone, Ayrshire]

ALEXANDER, HUGH., master of the Vanguard of Port Patrick trading with Donaghadee in 1819. [NRS.E504.29.17]

ALEXANDER, ROBERT, a skinner in Kilmarnock, Ayrshire, was admitted as a burgess and guilds-brother of Ayr on 11 September 1833, by right of his father Alexander Alexander, a skinner burgess and guilds-brother of Ayr. [ABR]

ALLAN, ANDREW, in Watersyde, testament, 1792, Comm. Glasgow. [NRS]

ALLAN, BRYCE, master of the <u>Albion of Greenock</u> from Glasgow with passengers bound for Quebec in 1846, from Greenock with passengers bound for Quebec in 1847, 1848. [BPP][GCA.TCN.26.2]

ALLAN, GEORGE, and William Steven, merchants in Kilmarnock, sequestration, 1803. [NRS.CS230.Seqn.A1.120]

ALLAN, HUGH, a merchant in Kilmarnock, Ayrshire, testament, 1790, Comm. Glasgow. [NRS]

ALLAN, HUGH, born 29 September 1810 in Ayrshire, son of Captain Alexander Allan, a merchant emigrated via Greenock aboard the <u>Favourite</u> bound for Canada on 12 April 1826. [BCC]

ALLAN, JAMES, born 1839, son of Alexander Allan, died in Chicago, Illinois, on 27 November 1876. [Whithorn gravestone, Galloway]

ALLAN, JOHN, a shipmaster in Greenock, Renfrewshire, testament, 1798, Comm. Glasgow. [NRS]

ALLAN, JOHN, a mariner in Greenock, testament, 1810, Comm. Glasgow. [NRS]

ALLEN, JOHN, was born in Irvine, Ayrshire, emigrated to New York, was admitted as a burgess of Irvine on 4 July 1851. [AA]

ALLAN, MARY MCKELVIE, born 1856, wife of William Clapperton, died in Pahi, Fiji, on 13 October 1896. [Greenock gravestone]

ALLAN, NEIL, a skipper in Greenock, 1804, Comm. Glasgow. [NRS]

ALLAN, PETER, born 1807, from Greenock, Renfrewshire, died in Pictou, Nova Scotia, on 18 November 1877. [GT.11.1.1878]

ALLAN, ROBERT, born 1786 in Kilbarchan, Renfrewshire, a poet who emigrated to America in April 1841, died in New York in 1842. [GM.ns18.331]

ALLASON, WILLIAM, a cooper in Hazletonhead, parish of Mearns, testament, 1791, Comm. Glasgow. [NRS]

ALLASON, WILLIAM, a messenger in Ayr, testament, 1793, Comm. Glasgow. [NRS]

ALLASON, WILLIAM, a carter at Slates, Paisley, Renfrewshire, testament, 1798, Comm. Glasgow. [NRS]

ALLASON, WILLIAM, master of the Jane Gordon of Ayr trading with Dublin in 1818. [NRS.E504.4.14]

ALLEN, JOHN, born in Irvine, Ayrshire, emigrated to New York, was admitted as a burgess of Irvine on 4 July 1851. [AA]

ALLEN, THOMAS, from Kirkbean, Galloway, was admitted to the Scots Charitable Society of Boston in 1819. [NEHGS/SCS]

ALLEN, Captain, master of the Monarch of Irvine from Glasgow with passengers bound for Quebec in 1842, and from Glasgow with passengers bound for Montreal in 1844. [GH.4.3.1842][SG.13.1341] [GCA.TCN.21/2][W.V.503]

AMOS, JAMES, in Jamaica, later in Moffat, Dumfries-shire, testament, 1828. [NRS.SC15.41.485]

ANDERSON, ALEXANDER, a merchant in Kilmarnock, sequestration, 1800. [NRS.CS230.SEQN.A.17]

ANDERSON, ALEXANDER, master of the Jean of Irvine from Greenock to Montreal in 1820, 1821, 1822. [NRS.E504.128/135/139]

ANDERSON, ANDREW, agent in Greenock, for the Union Bank of Scotland in 1849. [POD]

ANDERSON, DAVID, born 1782 in New Abbey, Galloway, an innkeeper, died in Portland parish, St John County, New Brunswick, on 9 July 1833. [NBC.13.7.1833]

ANDERSON, DAVID, born 1 July 1801 in Kilmarnock, Ayrshire, emigrated via Liverpool to America, landed in New York on 12 September 1821 aiming to settle in Philadelphia, Pennsylvania, was naturalised in New York on 15 December 1830. [NY Court of Common Pleas]

ANDERSON, EDWARD K., born 1803 in Galloway, a resident of Charleston, South Carolina, applied for naturalisation on 5 August 1830. [NARA.M1183.1]

ANDERSON, ELIZABETH, in Greenock, relict of Andrew Adam a merchant in Falkirk, testament, 1799, Comm. Glasgow. [NRS]

ANDERSON, JAMES ARNOT, in Newmilns, testament, 1792, Comm. Glasgow. [NRS]

ANDERSON, JAMES, born 5 November 1821 in Stoneykirk, Dumfries, son of Reverend James Anderson and his wife Mary McGhie, a vine grower who died in Valparaiso, Chile. [F.2.355]

ANDERSON, JANET, born 1763, relict of Matthew MacFarlane a farmer in Neilston, Renfrewshire, died in Broadle, Ramsay, Upper Canada, on 15 September 1844. [W.5.514]

ANDERSON, JOHN, formerly of the Honourable East India Company on Prince of Wales Island in the East Indies, later settled at Farthingrush, Dumfries-shire, in the 1820s. [NRS.CS231.Misc.20.3]

ANDERSON, Mrs MARGARET, born 1787, widow of David Anderson from Dumfries, died in Portland, St John, New Brunswick, on 25 April 1840. [NBC.25.4.1840]

ANDERSON, MATTHEW, agent of the Union Bank of Scotland in Barrhead, Renfrewshire, in 1849. [POD]

ANDERSON, ROBERT, in Borland, born 1750, died 11 May 1822. [Dunlop gravestone, Ayrshire]

ANDERSON, WILLIAM, a skipper in Greenock, master of the *Eliza*, testament, 1808, Comm. Glasgow. [NRS]

ANDERSON, WILLIAM, an Anti-Burgher and a grocer, was admitted as a burgess and guild-brother of Ayr on 8 September 1813. [ABR]

ANDERSON, WILLIAM, born 1808, son of William Anderson, died in Troy, USA, on 9 June 1842. [Westerkirk gravestone, Dumfriesshire]

ANDERSON, ..., master of the Hopewell of Dumfries trading with Ulverston in 1825. [NRS.E504.9.10]

ANDERSON, Captain, master of the Harmony of Irvine, from Troon, Ayrshire, bound for Quebec in 1849. [EEC.21870]

ANDREW, ELIZABETH, born 1818 in New Galloway, Kirkcudbrightshire, wife of Thomas Harper, died in New York on 15 December1855. [DGC.15.1.1856]

ANDREW, JOHN MCADAM, born 16 September 1807, son of John Andrew in Gillsburn, [1771-1856], and his wife Jean McAdam, [1780-1807], died in New York on 24 May 1835. [Kilmaurs gravestone, Ayrshire]

ANDREWS, JOHN, from Greenock, an employee of the Detroit and Michigan Railway, in Detroit, married Sarah C. Plummet in London, Canada, on 8 April 1859. [GA.5.5.1859]

ANDREWS, ROBERT, born 1858, son of William Andrews [1819-1914] and his wife Mary Milroy [1828-1908], died in Winnipeg on 27 October 1882. [Colmonell gravestone, Ayrshire]

ANDREW, THOMAS, farmer in Nether Borland, born 1766, died 15 December 1848, husband of Janet Anderson, born 1770, died 23 August 1856. [Dunlop gravestone, Ayrshire]

ANDREW, WILLIAM, in Shawhead, testament, 1791, Comm. Glasgow. [NRS]

ANDREWS, WILLIAM, agent in Girvan, Ayrshire, for the Union Bank of Scotland in 1849. [POD]

ARMOUR, JAMES, born 1821, a labourer, landed at Bluefields, Westmoreland, Jamaica, on 23 January 1841 from aboard the William Pirie from Stranraer, Wigtownshire. [TNA.CO.140.33]

ARMSTRONG, JAMES, born 1821, a carpenter, landed at Bluefields, Westmoreland, Jamaica, on 23 January 1841 from aboard the William Pirie from Stranraer, Wigtownshire. [TNA.CO.140.33]

ARMSTRONG, JANE, born 1817, from Garlieston, Sorbie, Wigtownshire, settled at Mount Pleasant, Saratoga County, New York, died there on 7 January 1859. [DGH.18.3.1859] [GW.17.3.1859]

ARMSTRONG, SARAH, born 1822, landed at Bluefields, Westmoreland, Jamaica, on 23 January 1841 from aboard the William Pirie from Stranraer, Wigtownshire. [TNA.CO.140.33]

ARMSTRONG, WILLIAM, born in Kirleton Gilnockie, Dumfriesshire, son of David Armstrong the Sheriff of Dumfries, a British Army officer from 1775 to 1783, settled in New York by 1790, died in Elizabethtown, New Jersey, on 27 January 1830. [ANY]

ARROL, WILLIAM, eldest son of William Arrol of Butts, Renfrewshire, married Sarah Jane Burt, eldest daughter of Darius Burt of Harwich, Upper Canada, there on 30 July 1849. [SG.1862]

ARTHUR, or CRAWFORD, THOMAS, of Cartsburn, testament, 1798, Comm. Glasgow. [NRS]

ASBRIDGE, PETER, master of the Royalist of Maryport from Greenock to New Brunswick in 1817 and 1819. [NRS.E504.15.117/125]

ASHCROFT, JAMES, born 1819, died 16 October 1845. [Riccarton gravestone, Ayrshire]

AUCHINCLOSS, JAMES, born 19 April 1794 in Paisley, Renfrewshire, son of James Auchencloss and his wife Jean Lyle, emigrated to New York in 1815, a merchant there, married Anna Steuart Shaw in 1821, died 17 October 1855. [ANY]

AULD, ADAM, a brewer in Irvine, Ayrshire, testament, 1793, Comm. Glasgow. [NRS]

AULD, W., master of the Margaret of Greenock from Greenock with passengers bound for New York in 1849. [NARA.M237.78]

AUSTIN, ADAM, from Milton, Moffat, Dumfries-shire, settled in Franklinville, Cattaraugus County, New York, before 1849. [DGH.2.8.1849]

BAILIFF, JOSEPH, born 1819, drowned near New York on 21 November 1836. [St Michael's gravestone, Dumfries]

BAILLIE, ELYSABETH, found guilty of theft in Dumfries and sentenced to transportation to the colonies for fourteen years, in 1814. [NRS.GD1.959]

BAIN, ALEXANDER, a farmer and former militiaman in Gourock, applied to settle in Canada on 5 June 1820. [TNA.CO384.6.125]

BAINE, ARCHIBALD, born 1796 in Greenock, died in Orilla, Canada, on 2 July 1854. [GA.4.8.1854]

BAIN, GEORGE, born 1790, a labourer in Greenock, emigrated via Port Glasgow on the Favourite of St John, bound for St John, New Brunswick on 22 October 1815. [PANB.ms.RS23E/9798]

BAIN, JOHN, a skipper in Greenock, testament, 1812, Comm. Glasgow. [NRS]

BAIN, LILIAS, widow of James Wilson a barber in Greenock, Renfrewshire, testament, 1798, Comm. Glasgow. [NRS]

BAIN, NICOL, a skipper in Greenock, testament, 1806, Comm. Glasgow. [NRS]

BAINE, ROBERT, agent in Greenock, for the Bank of Scotland in 1849. [POD]

BAIRD, DAVID, a merchant from Saltcoats, Ayrshire, married Margaret Boyd, youngest daughter of John Boyd, in St John, Newfoundland, on 23 August 1849. [SG.1861]

BAIRD, HUGH, a merchant in Rio de Janeiro, Brazil, son of Thomas Baird a merchant in Kilmarnock, Ayrshire, 1845. [NRS.S/H]

BAIRD, JOHN, agent in Lockerbie, Dumfries-shire, for the Edinburgh and Glasgow Bank in 1849. [POD]

BAIRD, WILLIAM, and his daughter Mary Baird, in Whitehill, Kelton, Kirkcudbrightshire, were victims of forgery and theft in 1850. [NRS.AD14.50.521]

BALDWIN, GEORGE, a merchant and shopkeeper in Paisley, Renfrewshire, a testament, 1790, Comm. Glasgow. [NRS]

BALLENTINE, JAMES, a mariner in Girvan, testament, 1810, Comm. Glasgow. [NRS]

BALLANTYNE, PATRICK, of Castlehill, son of William Ballantine, a merchant burgess and guild-brother of Ayr, was admitted as a burgess and guilds-brother there on 24 September 1800. [ABR]

BALLANTYNE, WILLIAM, a merchant in Ayr, testament, 1791, Comm. Glasgow. [NRS]

BALLINGALL, PATRICK, a barrister and city attorney, son of David Ballingall, MA, Rector of Ayr Academy, died in Chicago, Illinois, on 21 November 1858. [CM.21618]

BALSILLIE, JAMES, a cabinetmaker and joiner in Irvine, Ayrshire, sequestration, 1845. [NRS.CS280.31.7]

BANKS, Reverend JAMES, M.D., born 25 June 1803 in Irvine, Ayrshire, died in Saltcoats, Ayrshire, in 29 August 1890. [St Andrews gravestone, Kilmarnock, Ayrshire]

BANKS, JOHN, born 1763, son of John Banks a merchant in Kilwinning, Ayrshire, was educated at Glasgow University around 1787, a minister in Edinburgh, New York, and Montgomery County, Philadelphia, Pennsylvania, from 1816 until his death on 10 April 1826. [MAGU][UPC]

BARBOUR, ALEXANDER, tenant in Whitestanes, Beith, testament, 1794, Comm. Glasgow. [NRS]

BARBOUR, WILLIAM, born 31 March 1814 in Castle Douglas, Kirkcudbrightshire, son of Thomas Barbour and his wife Margaret

Cochrane, a merchant in New York, died at 11 West 32nd Street, N.Y., on 13 November 1885. [ANY]

BARCLAY, ANN, in Irvine, widow of Robert Barclay in the island of St Helena, afterwards wife of John Richardson late Captain of the Dragoons, now Captain Lieutenant of the Lanarkshire Cavalry, testament, 1799, Comm. Glasgow. [NRS]

BARCLAY, WILLIAM, master of the Britannia of Saltcoats from Greenock to Quebec in 1819. [NRS.E504.15.124]

BARR, JAMES, born 12 December 1752 in Kilbarchan, Renfrewshire, settled in Ipswich, New Hampshire, in 1773, died on 7 March 1829. [Imm.NE]

BARR, JOHN, a weaver in Paisley, later a soldier of the 94th Regiment of Foot, died in Spain, testament, Glasgow, 1813. [NRS]

BARR, JOHN, in Bridge of Weir, Renfrewshire, to emigrate to Upper Canada via Quebec in 1820. [NRS.SC58.75.79]

BARR, MARY, wife of John Barr in St Kitts, formerly in Greenock, died in New York on 11 March 1854. [GA.14.4.1854]

BARR, MATTHEW, born in Lochwinnoch, Renfrewshire, a baker who emigrated via Greenock to New York, naturalised there on 29 September 1818. [NY Court of Common Pleas]

BARR, ROBERT, in Bridge of Weir, Renfrewshire, to emigrate to Upper Canada via Quebec in 1820. [NRS.SC58.75.79]

BARRIE, CHRISTINA STEWART, born 1840, daughter of John Barrie and his wife Susannah Adams, wife of Alexander Stewart, died in Dunedin, New Zealand, on 30 April 1875. [Greenock gravestone, Renfrewshire]

BART, ABRAM, in Pennsylvania, a letter to Margaret Colquhoun in Paisley, Renfrewshire, dated 6 June 1834. [NRS.GD1.814.6.2]

BARTON, GEORGE M., born 1794 in Dumfries, a mason who died in Halifax, Nova Scotia, on 6 September 1843. [HT.12.9.1843]

BAXTER, ARCHIBALD, born 1823 in Greenock, Renfrewshire, emigrated to New York in 1856, a merchant who died in Brooklyn, N.Y., on 22 October 1884. [ANY]

BEATTIE, FRANCIS, born 1796, died in Port Hope, Upper Canada, on 29 September 1828. [Dumfries gravestone]

BEATTIE, GEORGE, a smith in Annan, Dumfries-shire, was accused of theft in 1842. [NRS.AD14.43.208]

BEATTIE, JAMES, born 1799 in Dumfries-shire, emigrated to New Brunswick in 1820, died from a fall from his horse at Truro, Nova Scotia, on 18 July 1822. [AR.27.7.1822]

BEATTIE, JAMES, born 1796, died in Port Hope, Upper Canada, on 29 September 1828. [Dumfries gravestone]

BEATTIE, JAMES C., born 1825 in Kells, Kirkcudbrightshire, died in New York on 11 November 1857. [DGH.11.12.1857]

BEATTIE, THOMAS, of Crieve, Dumfries-shire, born 1799, died in Madeira on 21 April 1836, buried in Funchal. [Westerkirk gravestone, Dumfries-shire] [ARM]

BEATTIE, WALTER, born 1789, from Ruthwell, Dumfries-shire, died in Iruxton, Cortland County, New York, on 23 February 1863. [AO]

BECK, JAMES, born 12 January 1814 in Dumfries, eldest son of Thomas Beck of Lincluden College Mains, emigrated to New York in 1834, a merchant and quartermaster of the Caledonian Fusiliers, died in N.Y. on 24 January 1853. [ANY]

BECK, JOHN, born 2 September 1817 in Dumfries, son of Thomas Beck, emigrated to New York in 1842, a merchant, married Janet Johnston from Dumfries-shire in 1853, died in Scotland on 13 November 1874. [ANY]

BECK, JOHN, son of William Beck in Balmangan, settled in New South Wales before 1857. [NRS.S/H]

BECK, JOSEPH, and his son Joseph Beck, coachbuilders in Dumfries, were accused of fire-raising in 1845. [NRS.AD14.45.149]

BECK, MARION, daughter of Thomas Beck of Lincluden College Mains, Dumfries-shire, married Charles Bathgate of Morrisiana, West Chester County, New York on 24 January 1853. [ANY]

BECK, WILLIAM, son of James Beck, [1770-1822], a carter in Dumfries, and his wife Sophia Bell, died in Quebec aged 29. [Dumfries gravestone]

BECK, WILLIAM JOHNSTON, born 14 May 1820 in Dumfries, son of Thomas Beck of Tynron, died at West Farms, New York, in April 1877. [ANY]

BEDDIE, BENJAMIN, son of David Beddie, a smith in Wigtown, manager of the Clare Valley Estate on St Vincent, died there on 28 September 1810. [Wigtown gravestone]

BEGGS, JOHN, a grocer in Stranraer, Wigtownshire, was accused of forgery in 1831. [NRS.A14.31.109]

BEGGS, THOMAS, born 1770 in Ayrshire, a merchant who died in Savanna, Georgia, on 11 September 1806. [Savanna Death Register]

BELL, Dr ALLAN, second son of Hugh Bell in Halfmerkland, Dalrymple, Ayrshire, died in Jamaica on 18 June 1845. [ASG.14.1424]

BELL, ANN, wife of Captain William Gordon, late of Greenock, died in Toronto, Ontario, on 29 July 1849. [SG.1851]

BELL, CHARLES, son of Benjamin Bell, [1764-1833], and his wife Jane Paton, died in Jamaica aged 43. [Dumfries gravestone]

BELL, CHRISTOPHER, born 6 July 1817 at Waulkmill, a flesher in Langholm, Dumfries-shire, died in Eastham, Cheshire, on 4 November 1895, husband of Isabella Dalgleish, born 1827, died 9 March 1860. [Wester Kirk, Dumfries-shire]

BELL, FRANCIS, of Carruthers, eldest son of John Bell a writer in Lockerbie, Dumfries-shire, died in Falmouth, Jamaica, on 27 January 1823. [DPCA]

BELL, GEORGE, son of George Bell in Dumfries, a writer in Edinburgh, was admitted as a Notary Public on 21 December 1799, later a writer in Ecclesfechan, Dumfries-shire, died 2 July 1836. [NRS.SC15.41.6.646]

BELL, HELEN, born 1807, emigrated via Stranraer, Wigtownshire, on the William Pirie bound for Jamaica, landed at Bluefields, Westmoreland, Jamaica, on 23 January 1841. [TNA.CO.140.33]

BELL, J., daughter of William Bell in Dumfries, and wife of Robert Wallace a painter in St John, New Brunswick, died in Glasgow on 18 January 1835. [CG.30.4.1845]

BELL, JAMES, born 1776, son of James Bell and his wife Mary Haugh in Dalton, Dumfries-shire, died at Morant Bay, Jamaica, on 10 November 1814. [Dalton gravestone]

BELL, JAMES, schoolmaster and Session clerk of Cathcart, Renfrewshire, in 1833. [NRS.CS228.B17.81]

BELL, JAMES, born 1835, an iron-moulder from Renfrewshire, emigrated via Glasgow on the Earl Granville on 16 March 1887 bound for Australia, landed at Bundaberg there on 13 July 1887. [BPP]

BELL, JOHN, born 1787, son of John Bell, [1756-1818], and his wife Ann Potter, [1755-1833], in Dumfries-shire, died in Spain on 12 August 1811. [Dornock gravestone, Dumfries-shire]

BELL, JOHN L., born 1792 in Dumfries, a merchant in New York, died on 26 January 1838. [ANY]

BELL, JOHN, in Annan, Dumfries-shire, applied to settle in Canada on 10 May 1827. [TNA.CO384.5.751]

BELL, JOHN, son of Robert Bell, was murdered at Balsmith Farm, Whithorn, Wigtownshire, in 1833. [NRS.AD14.33.348]

BELL, MARGARET, born 1809, emigrated via Stranraer, Wigtownshire, on the William Pirie bound for Jamaica, landed at Bluefields, Westmoreland, Jamaica, on 23 January 1841. [TNA.CO.140.33]

BELL, MARGARET, born 1815, emigrated via Stranraer, Wigtownshire, on the William Pirie bound for Jamaica, landed at Bluefields, Westmoreland, Jamaica, on 23 January 1841. [TNA.CO.140.33]

BELL, MARGARET, born 1819 in Dumfries-shire, widow of John Johnstone, died at 208 West Marshall Street, Richmond, Virginia, on 16 December 1897. [S.17015]

BELL, MARY ANN, second daughter of John Bell in Ruthwell, Dumfries-shire, wife of Alexander Hardgrave, died in New York on 27 October 1864. [AO]

BELL, RICHARD, son of Richard Bell in Tanlawhill, Dumfries-shire, died in New York in June 1857, testament, 1860. [NRS.SC70.1.103]

BELL, ROBERT, in New Abbey, Kirkcudbrightshire, applied to settle in Canada on 2 March 1815. [NRS.RH9]

BELL, THOMAS, messenger at arms, Maybole, Ayrshire, 1849. [POD]

BELL, WILLIAM, from Paisley, Renfrewshire, settled in Chester, New Hampshire, before 1780, married Beatrice Barr from Glasgow, died in 1817. [Imm.NE]

BELL, WILLIAM, born 1768, a farmer in Balmaghie, Stewartry of Kirkcudbright, with his wife Janet, born 1778, and five children, emigrated to Canada in 1818. [TNA.CO384.2]

BELL, WILLIAM, and his wife Jane, from Dumfries, parents of an infant son who died in Brooklyn Royal, New York, on 12 December 1854. [DGC.2.1.1855]

BIGGAR, ELIZABETH, from Dundrennan, Kirkcudbrightshire, died in Lewiston, Pennsylvania, on 14 October 1849. [DGH.17.1.1850]

BIGGAR, JOHN, born 1779 in Dumfries, son of John Biggar in Fourmerkland, a merchant who died in Greenwich, Kingston, Jamaica, on 25 June 1804. [Kingston gravestone][AJ.2957]

BIGGAR, JAMES, born 1789 in Dumfries, a merchant in Kingston, Jamaica, died there on 25 June 1814. [Kingston Cathedral gravestone]

BIGGAR, JOHN, from Dundrennan, Kirkcudbrightshire, died in Lewiston, Pennsylvania, on 7 October 1849. [DGH.17.1.1850]

BIGGAR, ROBERT, a tanner from Dumfries, now in America in 1790. [NRS.CS17.1.9/48]

BIGGART, WILLIAM, a farmer in Whitehill of Dalry, Ayrshire, testament, 1795, Comm. Glasgow. [NRS]

BIRD, JAMES, found guilty of theft in Dumfries and sentenced to transportation to the colonies for fourteen years, in 1815. [NRS.GD1.959]

BIRKMYRE, AGNES, relict of John Birkmyre a merchant in Paisley, Renfrewshire, testament, 1794, Comm. Glasgow. [NRS]

BISHOP, Mr, emigrated from Greenock aboard the Friends Captain Dunlop, bound for Jamaica, landed there in October 1794. [JRG.25.10.1794]

BLACK, ADAM, born 1798 in Kilmarnock, Ayrshire, died in Halifax, Nova Scotia, on 18 June 1842. [AR.18.6.1842]

BLACK, DUNCAN, a gabartman in Greenock, Renfrewshire, testament, 1800, Comm. Glasgow. [NRS]

BLACK, JAMES, a skipper in Greenock, testament, 1821, Comm. Glasgow. [NRS]

BLACK, JEAN GREY, from Dailly, Ayrshire, died in Canada in 1852. [GW.9.12.1852]

BLACK, JOHN, born 1810 in Greenock, Renfrewshire, a carpenter in Charleston, South Carolina, was naturalised there on 31 August 1832. [NARA.M1183.1]

BLACK, JOHN, born 1851 at Mennock Bridge, Sanquhar, Dumfries-shire, a soldier of the Royal Artillery, died at Meean Meer, India, on 12 August 1884. [S.12826]

BLACK, MARY ANN, born 1819, a labourer, emigrated via Stranraer, Wigtownshire, on the William Pirie bound for Jamaica, landed at Bluefields, Westmoreland, Jamaica, on 23 January 1841. [TNA.CO.140.33]

BLACK, WALTER, a shipmaster and merchant in Greenock, Renfrewshire, testament, 1791, Comm. Glasgow. [NRS]

BLACK, WILLIAM, from Ayrshire, died in Troy, Rensselear County, New York, on 19 January 1823. [DGC.10.2.1836]

BLACKBURNE, Mr, emigrated via Greenock on the brig Jane bound for Jamaica, arrived there in July 1794. [JRG.2.8.1794]

BLACKLOCK, ALEXANDER, from Annan, Dumfries-shire, settled in Prescott, Canada, deeds, 1853-1861. [NRS.B2/2.9.182; 10.178.11.69]

BLACKLOCK, ROBERT, born 1809, a shoemaker in Lockerbie, Dumfries-shire, was accused of assaulting and robbing Jean Dobie in High Street, Lockerbie, in 1830. [NRS.AD14.30.146]

BLACKLOCK, ..., master of the Isabella of Annan trading with Beaumaris in 1825. [NRS.E504.9.10]

BLAIN, ANDREW, born 1775 in Galloway, a wheelwright in Charleston, South Carolina, applied to be naturalised on 27 August 1813. [NARA.M1183.1]

BLAIN, JAMES, born 1799 in Ayrshire, died in Burton, Sunbury County, New Brunswick, on 11 May 1841. [NBC.22.5.1841]

BLAIR, ALEXANDER, born 1783, died in Quebec on 30 May 1810. [Dundonald gravestone, Ayrshire]

BLAIR, DAVID, possibly from Kirkcudbright, in Madeira, a letter, 1833. [NRS.GD1.884.25]

BLAIR, DAVID, born 1829, son of Joseph Blair and his wife Agnes McCreath, died in Belfast, Australia, on 19 July 1869. [Stewarton gravestone, Ayrshire]

BLAIR, Dr DUGALD, born 1815, son of James Blair a wine and spirit merchant in Greenock, Renfrewshire, died in St Stephen's, New Brunswick, on 23 December 1855. [GA.18.1.1856]

BLAIR, JOHN, born 1790, son of David Blair, [1760-1827], and his wife Jean Baker, [1766-1844], died in America in 1820. [Stewarton gravestone, Ayrshire]

BLAIR, MONCRIEF, an Anti-Burgher, was admitted as a burgess and guild-brother of Ayr on 12 September 1804. [ABR]

BLAIR, MONCRIEFF, of the Montreal Bank, son of Reverend John Blair in Colmonell, Ayrshire, died in October 1821. [S.5.258]

BLAIR, WILLIAM, born 1805 in Kirkcudbright, a resident of Charleston, South Carolina, applied for naturalisation on 21 March 1828. [NARA.M1183.1]

BLANCKEN, ISABELLA, born 1836, widow of John Cameron, died in Kilcreggan, Bunbury, Western Australia, on 8 May 1929. [Greenock gravestone, Renfrewshire]

BLANTYRE, Lord ALEXANDER, at Erskine, Renfrewshire, testament, 1794, Comm. Glasgow. [NRS]

BLOUNT, GEORGE, a cabinet-maker from Dumfries, died in New York on 28 October 1840. [DGH.10.12.1840]

BLOUNT, ROBERT, son of James Blount, [1756-1816], a farmer in Rosehall, and his wife Minnie Kissock, a surgeon who died in Jamaica on 23 July 1833. [Dumfries gravestone]

BLOUNT, SAMUEL, born 1794 in Dumfries, son of Lieutenant David Blount, died in St Thomas in the East, Jamaica, on 19 September 1828; inventory 1833. [Dumfries gravestone][Bath gravestone, Jamaica] [NRS.SC70.1.49]

BLYTH, JAMES, a pit oversman in Dalry, Ayrshire, died on 29 April 1864, father of Robert Blyth in Walhalla, Victoria, Australia. [NRS.S/H]

BOADEN, ROSANNAH, born 1795 in Largs, Ayrshire, widow of Andrew Ballantyne a cabinetmaker, in New Sneddon Street, Paisley, was accused of theft in 1831. [NRS.AD14.31.182]

BOG, THOMAS, a skipper in Greenock, testament, 1805, Comm. Glasgow. [NRS]

BOGLE, JOHN, born 1823, emigrated via Stranraer, Wigtownshire, on the William Pirie bound for Jamaica, landed at Bluefields, Westmoreland, Jamaica, on 23 January 1841. [TNA.CO.140.33]

BOGLE, MARY ANN, born 1818, a servant, emigrated via Stranraer, Wigtownshire, on the William Pirie bound for Jamaica, landed at Bluefields, Westmoreland, Jamaica, on 23 January 1841. [TNA.CO.140.33]

BOOTH,……., master of the Forthar of Dumfries trading with Ulverston in 1823. [NRS.AE504.9.10]

BOUCHIER, ALEXANDER, a merchant in Newfoundland, grandson of Alexander Buchier a skipper in Crawforddyke, Renfrewshire, a sasine, 1802. [NRS.RS81.23]

BORTHWICK, JOHN, born 1828, son of Thomas Borthwick and his wife Janet Murray, died in Cromore, North America, on 20 April 1869. [Westerkirk gravestone, Dumfries-shire]

BORTHWICK, MARGARET, born 1808 in Ayrshire, died and was buried in Madeira on 26 January 1847. [British Cemetery gravestone, Funchal]

BOSWELL, JAMES, of Auchenleck, Ayrshire, testaments, 1798, Comm. Glasgow. [NRS]

BOWATSON, Mrs ELIZABETH ANN, born 1790 in Kirkconnell, Dumfries-shire, wife of Charles Bowatson, died in St John, New Brunswick, on 28 February 1841. [STA.5.3.1841]

BOWES, DANIEL, master of the Providence Success of Maryport from Greenock to St John, New Brunswick in 1818 and 1819. [NRS.E504.15.122/123]

BOWIE, JAMES, a cotton spinner in Johnstone, Renfrewshire, was accused of discharging a firearm at Daniel Campbell in McDougall Street, Johnstone, in 1820. [NRS.AD14.20.2]

BOWIE, MARGARET, daughter of William Bowie in Ayr, relict of Major Robert Henderson of the 78th Highlanders, died in Kemptville, Upper Canada, on 6 September 1847. [AJ.5207] [EEC.21568]

BOWIE, WALKER, born 1830 in Greenock, Renfrewshire, died in New Orleans, Louisiana, on 5 February 1882. [GT.14.3.1882]

BOWIE, WILLIAM, late in Antigua, now in Ayr, son of John Bowie a merchant, burgess and guilds-brother of Ayr, was admitted as a burgess and guilds-brother of Ayr on 24 September 1790. [ABR]

BOWMAN, JOHN, son of John Bowman of Ashgrove, Ayrshire, died in Charleston, South Carolina, in 1807. [AJ.3120]

BOYD, ANN, daughter of Thomas Boyd of Pitcon, testament, 1793, Comm. Glasgow. [NRS]

BOYD, HELEN, born 1836, wife of James Bryden, died in Piston, Pennsylvania, on 3 April 1861. [Old Alloway gravestone, Ayrshire]

BOYD, HUGH, born 1821, arrived at Bluefields Westmoreland, Jamaica, on the William Pirie on 23 January 1841 from Stranraer, Wigtownshire. [TNA.CO140.33]

BOYD, JAMES W., son of Thomas Bell in Dumfries, died in St Mary's, Jamaica, on 15 October 1817. [AJ.3653]

BOYD, JANET, second daughter of James Boyd in Greenock, married William Caldwell from California, at Fishkill Landing, New York, on 21 February 1853. [GA.22.3.1853]

BOYD, MARGARET, daughter of Thomas Boyd of Pitcon, wife of James Wilson a bailie and merchant in Kilmarnock, Ayrshire, testament, 1793, Comm. Glasgow. [NRS]

BOYD, THOMAS, a tailor in Glasgow, testament, 1793, Comm. Glasgow. [NRS]

BOYD, THOMAS, former Deacon of the Coopers of Ayr, testament, 1794, Comm. Glasgow. [NRS]

BOYD, WILLIAM, formerly in Stevenston, lately in Saltcoats, Ayrshire, testament, 1796, Comm. Glasgow. [NRS]

BOYD, WILLIAM, born 1799 in Alloway, Ayrshire, a merchant in New York, married Mrs Agnes Crerar on 14 May 1835, died in N.Y. on 12 July 1864. [ANY]

BOYD, ..., master of the Martha of Dumfries trading with Ulverston in 1823. [NRS.E504.9.10]

BOYLE, JOHN, born 1818, a drawboy, in New Sneddon Street, Paisley, was accused of theft in 1831. [NRS.AD14.31.182]

BOYLE, JAMES, born 1817, a labourer in Pyehills, Ruthwell, Dumfriesshire, husband of Ann Hughes born in Londonderry, Ireland, was accused of bigamy with Margaret Farish, in 1847. [NRS.AD14.4.493]

BOYLE, BARNARD, a victim of assault etc. at the Old Foundry, West Hawkhill farm, St Quivox, Ayrshire, in 1843. [NRS.AD14.43.375]

BOYLE, WILLIAM, born 1816, son of Charles Boyle in Palmalley, Sorbie, Wigtownshire, was accused of the murder of John Bell, son of Robert Bell, at Balsmith Farm, Whithorn, Wigtownshire, in 1833. [NRS.AD14.33.348]

BRADY, MICHAEL, a victim of assault etc. at the Old Foundry, West Hawkhill farm, St Quivox, Ayrshire, in 1843. [NRS.AD14.43.375]

BRAND, DAVID, and his wife Janet …., parents of David Jollie Brand, born 1851, died in Narrows, Queensland, Australia, on 25 October 1897. [Greenock gravestone, Renfrewshire]

BRAND, JAMES, born 31 January 1822, son of James Brand, [1781-1840], and his wife Jean McQueen, a merchant in Ceylon, and later in New York, died there on 12 May 1897. [ANY][Dumfries gravestone]

BRAND, J., agent of the British Linen Company in Annan, Dumfries-shire, in 1849. [POD]

BREARCLIFFE, DONALD, born 1788, son of Matthew Brearcliffe, [1748-1824], and his wife Catherine……, [1750-1829], died in Jamaica on 24 October 1867. [Wigtown gravestone]

BRECKENRIDGE, WILLIAM, in Dowhill, Girvan, Ayrshire, testament, 1796, Comm. Glasgow. [NRS]

BRITON, ANDREW, messenger at arms, Cumnock, Ayr, 1849. [POD]

BROADFOOT, JAMES, born 1816, residing in College Street, Maxwelltown, Dumfries, husband of Janet Sloan, was accused of bigamously marrying Margaret Hannah, in 1849. [NRS.AD14.49.180]

BROADFOOT, ROBERT, in Whithorn, Wigtownshire, the victim of an assault in 1837. [NRS.AD14.37.218]

BROADFOOT, WILLIAM, from Galloway, a merchant in South Carolina, applied to be naturalised on 2 April 1798. [NARA.M1183.1]

BROADFOOT, WILLIAM, a merchant in Norfolk, Virginia, great grandson of John Broadfoot, a merchant in Wigtown, a sasine, 1799. [NRS.RS.Wigtown.544]

BRODIE, JOHN, from Knockmairshill, Greenock, settled in America by 1810. [NRS.CS17.1.29/326]

BRODIE, ROBERT, in Firhill, Lochwinnoch, Renfrewshire, father of Andrew James Brodie, born 1852, died in St Louis, Missouri, on 11 September 1873. [GH.10538]

BROWN, Lieutenant Colonel, of Bosseyreach, Jamaica, died in Annan, Dumfries-shire, on 7 June 1820. [SM.86.190]

BROWN, ALEXANDER, born in Greenock, Renfrewshire, died in Halifax, Nova Scotia, on 18 September 1826. [AR.23.9.1826]

BROWN, ANDREW, in Overhill, born 1719, died 15 March 1791, husband of Jean Anderson, born 1727, died 6 February 1801. [Dunlop gravestone, Ayrshire]

BROWN, ARCHIBALD, born 1787 in Paisley, Renfrewshire, son of Robert Brown a farmer, was educated at Glasgow University, emigrated to Demerara in 1818, a minister there from 1818 until 1824, died in Edinburgh in 1826. [F.7.674]

BROWN, COLIN, born 1846, died in Parramatta, Australia, on 2 June 1887. [Greenock, Renfrewshire, gravestone]

BROWN, DANIEL, born 1822 in North America, son of William Brown of the Hudson Bay Company, died in Kilmaurs, Ayrshire, on 9 November 1829. [Kilmaurs gravestone]

BROWN, DAVID, born in Sanquhar, Dumfries-shire, was educated at Edinburgh University, later a minister in Valcartier, Quebec, from 1833 until 1837. [F.7.628]

BROWN, ERSKINE, a skipper in Greenock, testament, 1808, Comm. Glasgow. [NRS]

BROWN, FRANCES, born 30 September 1805, daughter of William Brown in Kilmarnock, died in Lisbon, Portugal, on 6 April 1872, wife of Edward Medlicott. [Cemitario dos Inglezes, Lisbon]

BROWN, JAMES, born 1786 in Annan, Dumfries-shire, a minister in Calcutta, India, from 1823, died in Malacca, Malaya, on 23 September 1830. [St Andrew's Kirk, Calcutta, gravestone]

BROWN, JAMES, born 1787, son of Samuel Brown and his wife Mary Thomson, died in Jamaica on 12 July 1824. [Senwick gravestone, Kirkcudbrightshire]

BROWN, JAMES LUDOVICK, born 1828, son of William Brown, a merchant in Paisley, and his wife Mary Baird, died in Malaga, Spain, on 5 January 1856. [SGS]

BROWN, JAMES LOCKHART, of Greenock Grammar School, father of Dr James D. Brown who died in New York on 3 April 1875. [GA.1.5.1875]

BROWN, JANE, wife of Reverend W. B. Clark, formerly of Maxwelltown, Dumfries, died in Quebec on 16 February 1854. [W.XV.1525]

BROWN, JOHN, in Hill, born 1749, died 27 December 1829, husband of Agnes Gilmore, [1753-1786]. [Dunlop gravestone, Ayrshire]

BROWN, JOHN, master of the Dunlop of Greenock and Elizabeth Partelow, daughter of Jahiel Partelow jr. in St John, New Brunswick, were married there on 8 July 1821. [NBC.9.6.1821]

BROWN, JOHN, of Netherwood, Dumfries-shire, died in Richmond, Virginia, on 25 December 1822. [DPCA.1072]

BROWN, JOHN, born 1782, a weaver from Paisley, Renfrewshire, emigrated via Liverpool aboard the Mexico bound for America in 1830. [NWI]

BROWN, JOHN, born 17 June 1783, possibly second son of Andrew Brown in Stewarton, Ayrshire, was educated at Glasgow University, by 1819 he was a minister in Kingston, Jamaica, died on 17 March 1820. [F.7.669][St Andrews gravestone, Jamaica]

BROWN, JOHN, born 1821 in Dumfries-shire, a planter in Charleston, South Carolina, naturalised there on 5 July 1849. [NARA.M1183.1]

BROWN, J., master of the Eliza of Irvine from Troon, Ayrshire, bound for Dalhousie, New Brunswick, in 1843. [GA.5946]

BROWN, JOHN, born 1847, elder son of Malcolm Brown of Braehead, Saltcoats, Ayrshire, died at Montego Bay, Jamaica, on 25 June 1865. [Montego Bay gravestone, Jamaica]

BROWN, MALCOLM, minister at Kilbirnie, Ayrshire, testament, 1795, Comm. Glasgow. [NRS]

BROWN, MICHAEL, master of the Unity of Ayr trading with Belfast in 1818. [NRS.E504.4.14]

BROWN, ROBERT, a coast-waiter in Largs, Ayrshire, a decreet in 1829. [NRS.CS44.173.33]

BROWN, ROBERT STEELE, born 1832, son of Reverend Thomas Brown and his wife Janet Steele, died in Ballarat, Victoria, Australia, on 21 May 1908. [Inverkip, Renfrewshire, gravestone]

BROWN, SAMUEL, born 1779, son of Alexander Brown, [1737-1806], and his wife Agnes McGuffog, [1752-1828], died in Jamaica on 3 June 1803. [Senwick gravestone, Kirkcudbrightshire]

BROWN, WILLIAM, [1767-1854], and his wife Frances Hay, [1770-1848], parents of Matthew Brown who died in Australia on 21 November 1913. [Kilmarnock gravestone, Ayrshire]

BROWN, WILLIAM, born 1790 in Kilmaurs, Ayrshire, an employee of the Hudson Bay Company eventually Chief Trader from 1811 until his death on 19 March 1827. [HBRS.1.431][Kilmaurs gravestone]

BROWN, ..., master of the Jane of Dumfries trading with Ulverston in 1823. [NRS.E504.9.10]

BROWNING, JAMES, messenger at arms, Kilmarnock, Ayrshire, ,1849. [POD]

BRUCE, A. J., agent in Kilmarnock, Ayrshire, for the Commercial Bank of Scotland in 1849. [POD]

BRUCE, ARTHUR, born 1761, from Greenock, died in Geneva, USA, on 5 October 1843. [SG.1240]

BRUCE, JAMES, of Glencairn, born 1806, died at Turakina, Wellington, New Zealand, on 9 June 1884. [S.12812]

BRUCE, JAMES, an Anti-Burgher, and a maltster, son of David Bruce, a boatman and a burgess and guilds-brother of Ayr, was admitted as a burgess and guild-brother of Ayr on 19 September 1804. [ABR]

BRUNTON, ARCHIBALD, son of William Brunton, [1776-1841], and his wife Elizabeth Richardson in Tinwald, Dumfries-shire, died in Philadelphia, Pennsylvania, on 26 August 1839. [DGH.11.10.1839]

BRYDEN, JOHN, born 1800 in Dumfries-shire, died at Clark's Hill, Oneida County, New York, on 10 January 1875. [AO]

BRYDEN, WILLIAM, born 1816, gardener at Loch Ryan House, died 14 November 1871. [Cairnryan gravestone, Wigtownshire]

BRYDIE, JOHN, master of the Mary of Greenock, Renfrewshire, testament, 1796, Comm. Glasgow. [NRS]

BRYMER, JOHN FAIRLIE, born 1815, son of Alexander Brymer, [1788-1891], and his wife Isabella Fairlie, died in Quebec on 7 June 1829. [Greenock gravestone]

BRYSON, JOHN, a former soldier, residing at 153 Causeyside Street, Paisley, applied to settle in Canada on 1 May 1820. [TNA.CO384.6.117]

BUCHANAN, HECTOR DICK, married Margaret Boag Buchanan, eldest daughter of James Buchanan in Greenock, at 740 Riverside Drive, New York, on 15 October 1813. [GT.16.10.1813]

BUCHANAN or BLACK, JANET, in Paisley later in Rutherglen, mother of William Buchanan who settled in Melbourne, Victoria, Australia, before 1852. [NRS.S/H]

BUCHANAN, WILLIAM, possibly from Paisley, a saddler in Petersburg, Virginia, in 1809. [NRS.CS17.1.29/76]

BURGESS, GEORGE, from Galloway, died in Halifax, Nova Scotia, on 19 November 1829. [AR.21.11.1829]

BURGESS, WILLIAM, from Kells, Kirkcudbrightshire, died in New York on 31 May 1823. [DGH.9.7.1823]

BURNETT, JOHN JOSEPH, from Gadsgirth, Ayrshire, died in Naples, Italy, on 16 Mach 1862. [AJ.5960]

BURNS, JOHN, son of Thomas Burns a farmer in Fenwick, Ayrshire, was educated at Glasgow University in 1788, a minister of the Secession Church in Magara, USA, from 1803, died in 1822. [MAGU]

BURNS, ROBERT, a shipmaster in Greenock, Renfrewshire, testament, 1800, Comm. Glasgow. [NRS]

BURNS, ROBERT, from Fenwick, Ayrshire, a divinity student in 1792, a minister at Magara, USA, died in 1822. [AUPC]

BURNS, ROBERT, born in Dumfries, a mate in the United States Navy, died in Brooklyn Naval Hospital, New York, on 28 January 1865. [AO]

BURNS, WILLIAM, master of the Batchelor of Port Patrick trading with Donaghadee in 1819. [NRS.E504.29.17]

BURNS, Captain, master of the Favourite of Greenock from Greenock bound for Quebec in 1834. [MG][SG.3.270]

BURNSIDE, JAMES, born 18 April 1788 in Dumfries, son of Reverend William Burnside and his wife Anne Hutton, died in India in 1815. [F.2.267][St Michael's gravestone, Dumfries]

BURTT, JOHN, born 1790 in Kilmarnock, Ayrshire, served in the Royal Navy from 1806 until1811, later a weaver in Kilmarnock, and a teacher in Paisley, Renfrewshire, apolitical radical who went to America in 1817, was educated at Princeton University in New Jersey, became a Presbyterian minister in Salem, N.J. and in Blackwoodtown, N.J., died in Salem in 1866. [TSA]

BYERS, CHRISTIAN, born 1816, a farm servant from Billholm, Langholm, Dumfries-shire, emigrated to Australia in 1848. [BPP.11.598]

BYERS, HELEN, born 1823, a farm servant from Billholm, Langholm, Dumfries-shire, emigrated to Australia in 1848. [BPP.11.598]

CAIRD, JAMES, a writer from Stranraer, Wigtownshire, married Christian McNeil, second daughter of Archibald McNeil, in California on 9 October 1810. [SM.72.877]

CAIRNS, WILLIAM, of Torr in the Stewartry of Kirkcudbright, a merchant in New York in 1820. [NRS.CS17.1.39/203]

CALDER, DUNCAN, born 1800, from Greenock, died in Toronto, Ontario, on 14 June 1882. [GT.5.7.1882]

CALDERWOOD, DAVID, born 1718, a wright, died 23 May 1798, husband of Mary Douglas, born 1745, died 15 November 1803. [Riccarton gravestone, Ayrshire]

CALDERWOOD, JOHN, in Aiket, born 1772, died in December 1858, husband of Agnes Faulds, born 1769, died 10 September 1844. [Dunlop gravestone, Ayrshire]

CALDWELL, JAMES, born 1822 in Kilmarnock, Ayrshire, a merchant in New York by 1856, died there on 16 February 1862. [ANY]

CALDWELL, JOHN, a manufacturer in Paisley, Renfrewshire, absconded to New York before 1825. [NRS.CS236.Sederunt book 1/7]

CALDWELL, ROBERT, agent in Lochwinnoch, Renfrewshire, for the Western Bank of Scotland in 1849. [POD]

CAMBRIDGE, ARCHIBALD, a skipper in Greenock, testament, 1817, Comm. Glasgow. [NRS]

CAMERON, ANGUS, born 1768, a labourer from Auchenleck, Ayrshire, with his wife Ann Cameron, born 1781, and children Mary born 1803, and Euphemia born 1805, emigrated via Oban on the Clarendon of Hull, bound for Prince Edward Island, in August 1808. [TNA.CO.226.23]

CAMERON, JOHN, second son of John Cameron of Carntyne, parish of Barony, Glasgow, was educated at Glasgow University around 1767, died in Jamaica in 1794. [MAGU][Car.4.15]

CAMERON, JOHN, a weaver in Maxwellton Street, Paisley, President of the First Friendly Emigrant Society, applied to settle in Canada on 8 October 1827. [NRS.CO384.5.789]

CAMERON, MALCOLM, a cooper in Greenock, testaments, 1797-1798, Comm. Glasgow. [NRS]

CAMERON, WILLIAM, born 1844, a painter from Greenock, died in New York on 3 August 1881. [T.5.8.1881]

CAMPBELL, ABRAM, a steamboat agent in Stranraer, Wigtownshire, father of Patrick Campbell of the Oriental Bank in China, 1856. [NRS.S/H]

CAMPBELL, ALEXANDER, was admitted as a Freeholder of Renfrewshire on 20 January 1819.]NRS.CS31.17]

CAMPBELL, ALEXANDER MUIR, son of Matthew Campbell in Wigtown, an assistant surgeon who died in Nagpore, India, on 5 June 1820. [EEC]

CAMPBELL, ALEXANDER, born 1843, son of John Campbell and his wife Flora MacRae, died in Suva, Fiji, on 14 July 1892. [Greenock gravestone, Renfrewshire]

CAMPBELL, Mrs AMELIA, in Greenock, relict of John Campbell of Shirvan, testament, 1800, Comm. Glasgow. [NRS]

CAMPBELL, or FITZGERALD, Mrs ANN, daughter of John Campbell of Skerrington, testament, 1795, Comm. Glasgow. [NRS]

CAMPBELL, ARCHIBALD, a skipper in Greenock, testament, 1816, Comm. Glasgow. [NRS]

CAMPBELL, COLIN, born 1748, late Surveyor and Searcher of H.M. Customs in St John, New Brunswick, died in Cartside, Greenock, Renfrewshire, on 9 March 1814. [CG.1.8.1814]

CAMPBELL, COLIN, a skipper in Greenock, testament, 1810, Comm. Glasgow. [NRS]

CAMPBELL, DANIEL, in McDougall Street, Johnstone, Renfrewshire, a victim of a crime in 1820. [NRS.AD14.20.2]

CAMPBELL, ELIZABETH, born 1810, daughter of David Campbell, [1788-1848], and his wife Mary Porter, [1785-1868], died in New Orleans, Louisiana, on 1 September 1838. [Buittle gravestone, Kirkcudbrightshire]

CAMPBELL, GEORGE, a farmer in Chautague County, New York, a sasine, 1843. [NRS.RS Wigtown.4.16]

CAMPBELL, ISOBEL, spouse of Andrew Campbell a cotton manufacturer in Paisley, Renfrewshire, testament, 1800, Comm. Glasgow. [NRS]

CAMPBELL, JAMES, in Ayr, son of John Campbell of Horsecleugh, testament, 1791, Comm. Glasgow. [NRS]

CAMPBELL, JAMES, born 1 April 1825 in Greenock, died in Wallacetown, Canada, on 4 May 1882. [GT.20.5.1882]

CAMPBELL, JEAN, born 1788, daughter of David Campbell, [1756-1821], and his wife Janet McNish, [1756-1834], died in Delaware City, USA, on 13 November 1853. [Balmaghie gravestone, Kirkcudbrightshire]

CAMPBELL, JOHN, a farmer and former militiaman in Gourock, Renfrewshire, applied to settle in Canada on 5 June 1820. [TNA.CO384.6.125]

CAMPBELL, JOHN, born 1793, with his wife and nine children, in Symington, Ayrshire, applied to settle in Canada on 26 February 1827. [TNA.CO384.5.765]

CAMPBELL, MATTHEW, son of Matthew Campbell in Wigtown, died in Guelph, Upper Canada, on 25 October 1849. [EEC.211891]

CAMPBELL, PATRICK, a writer in Greenock, testaments, 1799-1800, Comm. Glasgow. [NRS]

CAMPBELL, PETER, found guilty of sheep stealing and was sentenced at Ayr to seven years transportation to the colonies in 1815. [NRS.GD1.959]

CAMPBELL, ROBERT, formerly a mariner in London, later in Barbieston, Dalrymple, Ayrshire, testament, 1794, Comm. Glasgow. [NRS]

CAMPBELL, ROBERT, found guilty of forgery and was sentenced at Ayr to transportation to the colonies in 1814. [NRS.GD1.959]

CAMPBELL, Captain ROBERT, born 1776 in Greenock, Renfrewshire, died in Georgia in 1818. [CMSA.1.4.1818]

CAMPBELL, T., messenger at arms in Greenock in 1849. [POD]

CAMPBELL, ROBERT, messenger at arms, Gatehouse of Fleet, Kirkcudbrightshire, 1849. [POD]

CAMPBELL, WILLIAM, of Fairfield, testament, 1791, Comm. Glasgow. [NRS]

CAMPBELL, WILLIAM, born in Kirkinner, Wigtownshire, in 1727, son of Reverend William Campbell and his wife Margaret Reid, a physician in Antigua who died in 1798. [F.2.365]

CAMPBELL, WILLIAM, born 1796, son of William Campbell, [1763-1816], and his wife Jane Herron, [1752-1835], died in New York in June 1850. [Crossmichael gravestone, Kirkcudbrightshire]

CANDLISH, WILLIAM, agent in New Galloway for the Edinburgh and Glasgow Bank in 1849. [POD]

CARNOCHAN, JANE, born in Galloway, settled in McIntosh County, Georgia, married William McMasters on 9 April 1826. [Daily Georgia, 11.4.1826]

CARNOCHAN, JOHN, born 1778 in Dumfries, emigrated to Nassau, Bahama Islands, settled in Georgia, married Harriet F. Putnam, parents of John Murray Carnochan, born 1812, died in 1841. [BLG]

CARNOCHAN, SAMUEL, born 1785, son of James Carnochan, [14-182], and his wife Sarah Houston, [1746-1785], died in Goderich, Ontario, on 5 March 1859. [Anwoth gravestone, Kirkcudbrightshire]

CARNOCHAN, WILLIAM, born 1774 in Gatehouse of Fleet, in the Stewartry of Kirkcudbright, settled in Darien, Georgia, in 1810, died there on 28 November 1825. [Daily Georgia.3.12.1825]

CARR, AGNES, daughter of J. Carr in Dumfries, and Adam Gordon from Aberdeen, were married in Pictou, Nova Scotia, on 20 September 1823. [HJ.22.9.1823]

CARR, ANDREW, born 1745 in Auchencairn, Kirkcudbrightshire, emigrated via London to New York in 1784, a shipbuilder who died in NY on 12 April 1812. [ANY]

CARR, JOSEPH, master of the William and James of Maryport from Greenock to Montreal in 1815. [NRS.E504.15.108]

CARRICK, ALEXANDER, born 1789 in Paisley, Renfrewshire, emigrated to USA in 1807, a merchant and manufacturer in New York and in New Jersey, died in Patterson, N.J. on 1 January 1834. [ANY]

CARRICK, ROBERT, born 1789 in Paisley, Renfrewshire, emigrated to USA in 1807, a merchant and manufacturer in New York and in New Jersey, died in Patterson, N.J. on 1 January 1867. [ANY]

CARRUTH, ROBERT, from Paisley, Renfrewshire, father of a son born at 631 3rd Avenue, New York, on 29 June 1874. [EC.28022]

CARRUTHERS, ELIZABETH, from Langholm, Dumfries-shire, and Thomas Smith a merchant tailor in Newcastle, New Brunswick, were married in Miramachi, N.B., on 29 January 1830. [GNS.2.2.1830]

CARRUTHERS, JAMES, born in Dumfries, a merchant in Savanna, Georgia, died in Augusta, Ga., on 9 September 1820. [CMSA.19.9.1820]

CARRUTHERS, JAMES, from Dumfries, and Eliza Harris from Aylesford, Nova Scotia, were married there on 14 November 1829. [AR.12.12.1829]

CARRUTHERS, JOSEPH, born 1783 in Scotland, settled in Savanna, Georgia in 1804, died 19 October 1823. [Daily Georgia.28.10.1823]

CARRUTHERS, MARY, born 1839, a nurse in Dumfries, landed in Hobart, Tasmania, Australia, from the White Star in 1855. [SRA.TD292]

CARRUTHERS, THOMAS, son of John Carruthers, [1734-1823], a joiner, and his wife Anne Haining, died in Jamaica aged 23. [Dumfries gravestone]

CARSAN, JANE MAXWELL, eldest daughter of William Carsan a writer in Dumfries, married John Kennedy from Upper Canada, youngest son of David Kennedy of Knocknalling, at Pleasance, Dumfries, on 10 April 1834. [SG.236]

CARSON, ANDREW, a merchant from Castle Douglas, Kirkcudbrightshire, who died in New York in May 1849. [DGH.26.7.1849]

CARSON, JOHN, and Isabella Proudfoot, both from Dumfries-shire, were married in St John, New Brunswick, on 23 July 1819. [NBC.24.7.1819]

CARSON, WILLIAM, messenger at arms in Wigtown, in 1849. [POD]

CARSON, ..., master of the Barbara of Dumfries trading with Ulverston in 1826. [NRS.E504.9.10]

CARSWELL, ALLAN, born 1794, from Colvend, Kirkcudbrightshire, died in East Worcester, Otsego County, New York, on 29 June 1833. [DGC.31.7.1833]

CARVILL, Captain, master of the Mary Ann of Greenock from Glasgow bound for New York in 1851. [S.1215]

CHALMERS, BRYCE, born 1796, probably from Galloway, an innkeeper in St David parish, Charlotte County, New Brunswick, died in August 1834, probate, 1834, N.B.

CHAPMAN, Dr NATHANIEL, a physician in Philadelphia, Pennsylvania, was admitted as a burgess and guilds-brother of Ayr on 4 October 1802. [ABR]

CHESIRE, ROBERT, a land waiter in Saltcoats, Ayrshire, testament, 1796, Comm. Glasgow. [NRS]

CHILLAS, DAVID, third son of Robert Chillas in Paisley, Renfrewshire, died in New York on 21 August 1843. [SG.1243]

CLARK, Mrs AGNES, born 1756 in Kirkcudbright, widow of James Clark, died in Halifax, Nova Scotia, on 12 June 1826. [AR.17.6.1826]

CLARK, DAVID, born in Auchencairn, Kirkcudbrightshire, a lumber merchant in New York from 1799 to 1833, married Mary Buchan in February 1803, died in N.Y. on 30 December 1835. [ANY]

CLARK, DUNCAN, a porter in Greenock, Renfrewshire, testament, 1794, Comm. Glasgow. [NRS]

CLARK, ISABELLA, daughter of William Clark in Scarborough, Upper Canada, from Beith, Ayrshire, married William Young of the township of Markham, in Scarborough, U.C., on 5 November 1846. [W.VII.739]

CLARK, JAMES, a feuar in Largs, Ayrshire, testament, 1798, Comm. Glasgow. [NRS]

CLARK, JOHN, born near Irvine, Ayrshire, a private of the 34th Regiment, died in St John, New Brunswick, on 31 December 1832. [NBC.5.1.1833]

CLARK, JOHN, eldest son of Robert Clark of Clark's Mill, Oneida County, New York, late of Windmill, Annan, Dumfries-shire, died in Hartford, Connecticut, on 2 March 1864. [AO]

CLARK, JOHN, born 1779, son of Margaret Scott or Clark, [1758-1855], settled in Louisiana, died in Maxwelltown, Dumfries, on 9 April 1866. [Dumfries gravestone]

CLARK, THOMAS, born 1772, a farmer in Lochwinnoch, Renfrewshire, emigrated via Greenock on the William of New York bound for New York on 4 September 1817, landed there on 17 October 1817. [NY Municipal Archives][NY Commercial Advertiser, 18.10.1817]

CLARK, ROBERT, master of the Industry of Dumfries trading with Ulverston in 1823. [NRS.E504.9.10]

CLARK, WILLIAM, a victim of assault etc. at the Old Foundry, West Hawkhill farm, St Quivox, Ayrshire, in 1843. [NRS.AD14.43.375]

CLAYTON, THOMAS, from Potterhill, Paisley, Renfrewshire, died in Poplar Grove, Wilmington, North Carolina, on 1 October 1793. [GM.63.1214]

CLELLAND, JOHN, in Whithorn, Wigtownshire, the victim of an assault in 1837. [NRS.AD14.37.218]

CLEMENTSON, THOMAS, in Annan, Dumfries-shire, sequestration, 1841. [NRS.CS279.490]

CLENAHAN, ROBERT, born 1805, a house servant in Balmaclellan, Kirkcudbrightshire, was accused of theft in 1824. [NRS.AD14.24.150]

CLIENCOFF, JOHN, a weaver in Glasgow, son of Jacob Cliencoff, a sugar baker in Glasgow, and his wife Mary Lawson, was admitted as a burgess and guilds-brother of Ayr on 24 April 1822, by right of his mother Mary

Lawson, daughter of Hugh Lawson, a cooper burgess and guilds-brother of Ayr. [ABR]

COATS, ANDREW, born 22 June 1814 in Paisley, Renfrewshire, son of James Coats, a thread manufacturer, and his wife Catherine Mitchell, was educated at Edinburgh University, a merchant in New York and Philadelphia from 1839 to 1860, died in Perth on 10 February 1900. [ANY][AP]

COATS, Dr DAVID, born 1817 in Paisley, Renfrewshire, son of James Coats and his wife Catherine Mitchell, emigrated to USA in 1839, settled in New York and Philadelphia, died at 20 Bleecker Street, N.Y., on 18 May 1856. [ANY]

COATS, JAMES, a skipper in Greenock, testament, 1812, Comm. Glasgow. [NRS]

COCHRAN, ALEXANDER, born 1792, in West Grange, died 28 October 1875, husband of Margaret Robertson, born 1793, died 22 May 1848. [Dunlop gravestone, Ayrshire]

COCHRAN, ANDREW, born 1754, died in 1821, son of William Cochran and his wife Margaret Fulton, [1712-1780]. [Dunlop gravestone, Ayrshire]

COCHRAN, CHARLES PATTERSON, born 6 January 1804 in Kirkcudbright, son of Robert Cochrane and his wife Elizabeth Guthrie, was educated at Edinburgh University, a physician in Jamaica from 1825 to 1834, later a merchant in New York, died there on 28 December 1869. [ANY]

COCHRAN, FERGUS, born December 1804 in Kirkcudbright, son of Robert Cochrane and his wife Elizabeth Guthrie, a merchant in New York by 1830, died in St Croix, Danish West Indies, on 8 December 1831. [ANY]

COCHRAN, JAMES BLAIR, born 25 November 1799 in Kirkcudbright, son of Robert Cochrane and his wife Elizabeth Guthrie, later an import merchant in New York from 1831, died in Sing Sing, N.Y., on 25 April 1859. [ANY][DGH.13.5.1859]

COCHRANE, JAMES, in Crosslets, Paisley, a former Sergeant of the 94th Regiment of Foot, with his wife and four children, applied to settle in Canada on 4 January 1827. [TNA.CO384.5.761]

COCHRANE, JOHN, of Clippins, Kilbarchan, Renfrewshire, testament, 1794, Comm. Glasgow. [NRS]

COCHRAN, ROBERT, born 9 May 1788 in Kirkcudbright, son of Robert Cochrane and his wife Elizabeth Guthrie, a merchant in New York, in Natchez, Mississippi, around 1845, 'many years a resident in New York', died in Albany, N.Y., on 30 July 1849. [ANY][SG.1847][DGH.23.8.1849]

COCHRAN, ROBERT, in Loanhead, born 1768, died 14 August 1836, husband of Jean Andrew, born 1771, died 1803. [Dunlop gravestone, Ayrshire]

COCHRAN, SAMUEL, born 23 February 1806 in Kirkcudbright, son of Robert Cochrane and his wife Margaret (?) Guthrie, a merchant in New York, died at Dobbs Ferry, N.Y., on 31 August 1859. [ANY][DGH.23.9.1859]

COCHRANE, THOMAS, born 1760, died 26 May 1829, husband of Jean Stevenson, who died on 20 May 1840. [Dunlop gravestone, Ayrshire]

COCHRAN, THOMAS, born 1802, son of Robert Cochran, [1745-1829] and Jean ...., [1748-1829], died in Jamaica on 26 September 1853. [Dunlop gravestone, Ayrshire]

COCHRANE, THOMAS, born 2 June 1807 in Kirkcudbright, son of Robert Cochrane and his wife Margaret Guthrie, a lace merchant in New York, died in N.Y., on 28 November 1889. [ANY]

COCHRANE, WILLIAM, born 1784, son of Captain William Cochrane and his wife Agnes in Greenock, Renfrewshire, died in the St Lawrence River, Quebec on 31 August 1803. [GM.73.1254] [Inverkip gravestone]

COLLINS, GRACE, a seamstress from Paisley, Renfrewshire, landed in Hobart, Tasmania, Australia, from the Conway on 14 October 1855. [SRA.TD292]

COLLINS, JOHN, a labourer from Paisley, Renfrewshire, landed in Hobart, Tasmania, Australia, from the Conway on 14 October 1855. [SRA.TD292]

COLLINS, PATRICK, a seaman aboard the William of Greenock, testament, 1809, Comm. Glasgow. [NRS]

COLTART, JAMES, born 1815, son of William Coltart, [1758-1836], and his wife Marion Good, [1776-1827], died in Canada West on 1 August 1887. [Balmaclellan gravestone, Dumfries-shire]

COLTART, MARY, born 1818, daughter of William Coltart, [1758-1836], and his wife Marion Good, [1776-1827], died in Paris, Brantford township, Upper Canada, on 15 August 1847. [Balmaclellan gravestone, Dumfries-shire]

COLTART, RODGER, born 1767, son of William Coltart of Bluehill, [1721-1772], and his wife Catherine Kirkpatrick, [1734-1807], late in Virginia, died 1803. [Buittle gravestone, Wigtownshire]

COLTART, SEPH, born 1809, son of James Coltart in North Glen, [1781-1861], and his wife Marion Coltart, [1782-1855], died in California on 29 October 1851. [Buittle gravestone, Wigtownshire]

CONN, MARTIN, born 1814, of George Street, Content, Ayrshire, was, with others, accused of murder, mobbing, rioting, and assault with firearms at the Old Foundry, West Hawkhill farm, St Quivox, Ayrshire, in 1843. [NRS.AD14.43.375]

COOK, JOHN, born 13 April 1805 in Sanquhar, Dumfries-shire, was educated at Glasgow and Edinburgh Universities, a minister and academic in Quebec and Ontario from 1836, died in Quebec on 1 April 1892. [F.7.631]

COOK, Captain NEIL, a resident of Greenock, master of the Rover of Glasgow, testaments, 1797-1800, Comm. Glasgow. [NRS]

COPLAND, JOHN, master of the sloop Jane of Dumfries, testament, 1825, Comm. Dumfries. [NRS]

COPLAND, MAXWELL, a mariner in Hallgreen, testament, 1825, Comm. Dumfries. [NRS]

CORRIE, THOMAS, a messenger at arms in Dumfries in 1849. [POD]

COSKRY, NATHANIEL, born in Keltonhill, Kirkcudbrightshire, a hosier and haberdasher in New York from 1807, died at sea in August 1811. [ANY]

COSKRY, SAMUEL, born 1797, in Keltonhill, Kirkcudbrightshire, emigrated to USA by 1830, a merchant in New York, died on 17 October 1835. [ANY]

COULTER, DAVID, son of William Coulter, [1805-1875], and his wife Mary McBryde, [1810-1853], died in Trinidad aged 34. [Ballantrae gravestone, Ayrshire]

COULTER, JAMES, born 1806, a weaver in Elleslie, Kirkmahoe, Dumfries-shire, was accused of poaching in 1832. [NRS.AD14.32.81]

COULTER, WILLIAM, born 1805, died in Ballantrae on 25 May 1875, husband of Mary McBryde, born 1810, died 23 March 1863, parents of John Coulter who died in Australia aged 40, and David Coulter, died in Trinidad aged 34. [Ballantrae gravestone, Ayrshire,]

COULTHARD, CHRISTOPHER, a constable, Woodhouse, Canonbie, Dumfries-shire, deceased by 1829. [NRS.AD14.29.220]

COUPAR, JOHN, born 1759, son of Reverend John Coupar, [1706-1787], in Lochwinnoch, Renfrewshire, settled in Hopeton, St Simon's Island, Georgia in 1804, died in 1850. [UNC; Coupar pp]

COUPLAND, ..., master of the Grace of Dumfries trading with Ulverston in 1823. [NRS.E504.9.10]

COWAN, JAMES, born 1787 in Dumfries-shire, a stonecutter who settled in St John, New Brunswick, in 1819, died there on 2 .104]

COWAN, JAMES, a candlemaker in Irvine, 1845. [NRS.GD1.500.14]

COWAN, PATRICK, agent of the Clydesdale Bank in Ayr, in 1849. [POD]

COWAN, THOMAS, in Netherton, Allmurness, Buittle, Kirkcudbrightshire, a victim of theft in 1824. [NRS.AD14.24.150]

COWAN, WILLIAM, in Maxwelltown, Troquier, Stewartry of Kirkcudbright, was accused of housebreaking, theft, and reset at Hall of Drumpark, Irongray, Kirkcudbrightshire, in 1832. [NRS.AD14.32.57]

COWAN, ..., master of the Lively of Dumfries trading with Whitehaven in 1825. [NRS.E504.9.10]

COWIE, ADAM, agent in Kilmarnock, Ayrshire, for the Bank of Scotland in 1849. [POD]

CRAIG, CHARLES XAVIER, an artist and engraver in Hoboken, New Jersey, heir to his uncle John Craig, jr., a bank accountant in Dumfries, who died on 30 January 1848, re property in Castle Douglas, Kirkcudbrightshire. [NRS.S/H]

CRAIG, JAMES, a cotton spinner in Johnstone, Renfrewshire, was accused of discharging a firearm at Daniel Campbell in McDougall Street, Johnstone, in 1820. [NRS.AD14.20.2]

CRAIG, JOHN, of Lownsdale Abbey, Paisley, Renfrewshire, testaments, 1789-1790, Comm. Glasgow. [NRS]

CRAIG, PETER, master of the Jane of Ayr from Greenock to Quebec in 1814; master of the Saltcoats of Saltcoats from Greenock to Montreal in 1815. [NRS.E504.15.104/108]

CRAIG, ROBERT, of Lownsdale, testament, 1791, Comm. Glasgow. [NRS]

CRAIG, ROBERT, son of Robert Craig of Giffin, Beith, Ayrshire, a merchant in Manchester, Virginia, in 1800. [NRS.CS17.1.18/397; CS18.715.2]

CRAIG, ROBERT, born 1798, died 15 September 1873. [Dunlop gravestone, Ayrshire]

CRAIG, ROBERT, schoolmaster of Dreghorn, Ayrshire, a decreet, 1828. [NRS.CS44.162.34]

CRAWFORD, ARCHIBALD, a merchant in Greenock, testament, 1799, Comm. Glasgow. [NRS]

CRAWFORD, DAVID ROSE, born 1829, a solicitor from Greenock, Renfrewshire, died in New York on 6 October 1877. [EC.29035][S.10687]

CRAWFORD, Lieutenant Colonel HENRY, youngest son of Archibald Crawford in Greenock, died at San Sebastian, Spain, in 1813. [SM.76.78]

CRAWFORD, JAMES, [1810-1863], and his wife Margaret Mitchell, [1811-1856], parents of John Crawford and Robert Crawford in Paterson, New Jersey. [Old Cumnock gravestone, Ayrshire]

CRAWFORD, JAMES, agent of the Western Bank in Cumnock, Ayrshire, in 1849. [POD]

CRAWFORD, JAMES, born 1815, son of Hugh Crawford, [1782-1866], a farmer in Galston, Ayrshire, and his wife Euphemia White, [1788-1878], died in Delaware on 29 August 1848. [Loudoun gravestone, Ayrshire]

CRAWFORD, JEAN, in Old Cumnock, Ayrshire, daughter of James Crawford, a merchant in Dalmellington, Ayrshire, and his wife Sarah Mitchell, testament, 1795, Comm. Glasgow. [NRS]

CRAWFORD, Lieutenant Colonel JOHN WALKINGSHAW, of Crawfordland, testament, 1793, Comm. Glasgow. [NRS]

CRAWFORD, JOHN HUNTER SPREULE, of Cowdenhill, testament, 1795, Comm. Glasgow. [NRS]

CRAWFORD, JOHN, a mariner in Crawforddyke, testament, 1807, Comm. Glasgow. [NRS]

CRAWFORD, JOHN, in Paisley, Renfrewshire, and his wife Jean Whyte who died on 15 January 1829, great-grand parents of John Crawford, a farmer in Bullanto, Victoria, Australia. [NRS.S/H]

CRAWFORD, LAWRENCE, born 1787, a weaver from Paisley, emigrated via Liverpool aboard the <u>Mexico</u> bound for America in 1830. [NWI]

CRAWFORD, MARGARET, married George Steineth Harding from St Croix in the Danish West Indies, in Fairfield, Ayrshire, on 26 August 1811. [DPCA.476]; she died in St Croix in October 1835. [Logie gravestone, Stirling]

CRAWFORD, Captain MOSES, a fear in Irvine, Ayrshire, later in Virginia by 1797. [NRS.CS17.1.16/131]

CRAWFORD, PETER, son of Peter Crawford in Barbieston, Ayrshire, died in New York, on 5 September 1843. [SG.II.1239]

CRAWFORD, THOMAS, of Cartsburn, Renfrewshire, testament, 1791, Comm. Glasgow. [NRS]

CRAWFORD, WILLIAM, of Cartsburn, was admitted as a Freeholder of Renfrewshire on 1 July 1818.]NRS.CS32.17.1]

CREIGHTON, ROBERT, in Dumfries, a victim of arson in 1845. [NRS.AD14.46.301]

CRICHTON, JAMES, a barber in Paisley, Renfrewshire, testament, 1797, Comm. Glasgow. [NRS]

CRICHTON, ROBERT, a skipper in Irvine, Ayrshire, testament, 1815, Comm. Glasgow. [NRS]

CRICHTON, THOMAS, a stone dyker in Minniehive, Glencairn, Dumfries-shire, was accused of poaching in 1827. [NRS.JC26.1827.130]

CRICHTON, WILLIAM, from Glencairn, Dumfries-shire, settled at the Cape of Good Hope, South Africa, by 1830, a decreet. [NRS.CS46.1830.155]

CRON, ROBERT, son of John Cron and his wife Janet Craik in Torthorwald, Dumfries-shire, emigrated to the West Indies, father of Anna, Elizabeth, and Jessy who died and were buried in Jamaica in 1831. [Torthorwald gravestone]

CROOKS, RAMSAY, born 28 January 1786 in Greenock, Renfrewshire, a fur trader and explorer in Oregon and Washington, later a merchant and insurance company director in New York, died in New York on 8 January 1859. [ANY]

CROSBIE, JAMES, born 1794 in Sanquhar, Dumfries-shire, died in New York on 18 June 1858. [DGH.9.7.1858]

CROSBIE, MARGARET, born 1824, daughter of William Crosbie a gardener in Dalskairth, Troqueer parish, Kirkcudbrightshire, died in New York on 20 November 1843. [DGH.21.12.1843]

CROSS, ROBERT, of Greenlaw, Paisley, testament, 1797, Comm. Glasgow. [NRS]

CROSS, WILLIAM, born 1751 in Paisley, Renfrewshire, settled in Nova Scotia around 1783, died in Annapolis Royal, N.S., on 4 August 1834. [NBC.23.8.1834]

CRUMPS, WILLIAM, born 1792, son of John Crumps, died 23 June 1813. [Riccarton gravestone, Ayrshire]

CULBERT, THOMAS, an Excise officer in Ochiltree, Ayrshire, and his wife Jean Edgar, testament, 1795, Comm. Glasgow. [NRS]

CUMMING, JACOBINA, born 1833, daughter of John Cumming [1800-1879], and his wife Elizabeth Bell, [1807-1868], wife of James Russell, died in Canada on 28 January 1868. [Maybole gravestone, Ayrshire]

CUMMING, JOHN GILROY, MD, son of John Cumming a teacher in Greenock, died in New York on 29 January 1846. [W.VII.654]

CUMMING, ROBERT, a skinner in Kilmarnock, Ayrshire, testament, 1792, Comm. Glasgow. [NRS]

CUMMING, WILLIAM, master of the Sally of Ayr from Greenock to Quebec and Montreal in 1820. [NRS.E504.15.128]

CUNNINGHAM, ANDREW, jr., born 1808 in Dumfries-shire, died at Gardner's Creek, New Brunswick, on 30 March 1833. [WO.16.1833]

CUNNINGHAM, GORDON, born 1808, a besom maker in Maxwelltown, Troquier, Stewartry of Kirkcudbright, was accused of housebreaking, theft, and reset at Hall of Drumpark, Irongray, Kirkcudbrightshire, in 1832. [NRS.AD14.32.57]

CUNNINGHAM, Mrs JANET, widow of James McGhie, wife of Gordon Cunningham, in Maxwelltown, Troquier, Stewartry of Kirkcudbright, was accused of housebreaking, theft, and reset at Hall of Drumpark, Irongray, Kirkcudbrightshire, in 1832. [NRS.AD14.32.57]

CUNNINGHAM, ROBERT, born 1808, son of Andrew Cunningham [1756-1819], and his wife Jane McCraith, [1783-1814], died in Talcahuano, Chile, on 6 August 1877. [Barr gravestone, Ayrshire]

CUNNINGHAM, THOMAS SMITH, in Caprington, born 11 May 1813, died 30 June 1857. [Riccarton gravestone, Ayrshire]

CUNNINGHAM, WILLIAM, a mason in Paisley, Renfrewshire, testament, 1791, Comm. Glasgow. [NRS]

CUNNINGHAM, Sir WILLIAM, in Caprington, born 19 December 1752, died 16 January 1829. [Riccarton gravestone, Ayrshire]

CURDY, WILLIAM, master of the <u>Mary of Ayr</u> trading with Dublin in 1818. [NRS.E504.4.14]

CURRIE, JOHN, born 1762 in Galloway, settled in Savanna, Georgia, died 27 September 1799, buried in the Old Colonial Cemetery there. [CMSA.1.10.1799][Savanna gravestone]

CURRIE, WILLIAM, born 1808, from Crocketfield, Kirkcudbrightshire, died in Lynden Cattaraugus County, New York, on 10 October 1858. [DGH.9.11.1858]

CURRIE, WILLIAM, born 1825, son of Captain William Currie in Greenock, died in Madeira on 29 October 1846. [ARM]

CUTHBERT, ARTHUR ANDREW, from Ayr, married Emily Selina Fawcett, daughter of Colonel William Fawcett of London, at Schroon Lake, Warren County, New York, on 17 August 1861. [S.1947]

CUTHBERTSON, MARGARET, born 1814, daughter of David Cuthbertson and his wife Jane Rankin, died in Canada on 12 April 1866. [Kilmaurs gravestone, Ayrshire]

CUTHBERTSON, Reverend WILLIAM, born in December 1837 in Paisley, Renfrewshire, ordained into the United Presbyterian Church in Portadown, Ireland, in 1868, a minister in Kilmarnock, Ayrshire, from 1875 until his death on 25 October 1891, husband of Barbara Martin Cunningham, who died in Glasgow on 3 October 1932. [Kilmarnock cemetery, Ayrshire]

CUTHILL, WILLIAM, a skipper in Greenock, testament, 1807, Comm. Glasgow. [NRS]

DALGLEISH, ..., master of the Henrietta of Dumfries trading with Ulverston in 1826. [NRS.E504.9.10]

DALLING, MARY, born 1794, daughter of John Dalling in Boatcroft, [1761-1831], died in White Pigeon, USA, in October 1854. [Balmaghie gravestone, Kirkcudbrightshire]

DALLING, ROBERT, born 1797, son of John Dalling in Boatcroft, [1761-1831], died in St Elizabeth's, Jamaica, in October 1854. [Balmaghie gravestone, Kirkcudbrightshire]

DALMAHOY, NINIAN, master of the Rachel of Greenock, testament, 1815, Comm. Glasgow. [NRS]

DALYELL, JOHN, from Glenroan, Crossmichael, Dumfries-shire, died in Delaware on 18 October 1838. [DGC.26.8.1838]

DALZIEL, JAMES, born 1808, master of the wherry New Union of Dumfries, residing in Maxwelltown, Dumfries, was accused of theft in 1842. [NRS.AD14.42.407]

DARROCH, DUNCAN, a labourer in Ardrossan, Ayrshire, was accused of rape in April 1817, trial papers. [NRS.JC26.1817.225]

DAVIDSON, ALEXANDER, in Moss Street, Paisley, a victim of theft in 1831. [NRS.AD14.31.182]

DAVIDSON, ANDREW, in Burnhead, Cottage, Lockerbie, Dumfries-shire, father of David S. Goodburn Davidson, born 1852, died in Brewster, Putnam, New York, on 20 March 1878. [AO]

DAVIDSON, ISAAC, born 25 July 1804 in Sorbie, Wigtownshire, son of Reverend Elliot W. Davidson and his wife Mary McTaggart, a surgeon in the Service of the East India Company, died on 25 June 1833. [F.2.377]

DAVIDSON, JAMES W., born 1820, died in Newfoundland on 14 April 1837. [Anwoth gravestone, Kirkcudbrightshire]

DAVIDSON, JAMES, born 22 December 1826, son of John Davidson and his wife Elizabeth McGregor, died at Boemly Creek, New South Wales, Australia, in August 1869. [Glencairn gravestone, Dumfries-shire]

DAVIDSON, J., agent of the Clydesdale Bank in Ayr, in 1849. [POD]

DAVIDSON, JOHN, a student at the Scots College in Valladolid, Spain, in 1780, died in Greenock on 8 January 1815. [RSC]

DAVIDSON, ROBERT T., born 1811, died in Texas on 1 April 1836. [Anwoth gravestone, Kirkcudbrightshire]

DAVIDSON, WILLIAM, from Kilmarnock, Ayrshire, died in Georgia on 14 December 1801. [CMSA.18.12.1801]

DAVIDSON, WILLIAM, jr., born 1799 in Dumfries-shire, a merchant in Charleston, South Carolina, was naturalised there on 6 May 1834. [NARA.M1183.1]

DAVIDSON, Captain, master of the Catherine of Irvine from Irvine, Ayrshire, to Quebec in 1832. [GA.4261][QM.2.6.1832]

DAWSON, JOHN, a victim of assault etc. at the Old Foundry, West Hawkhill farm, St Quivox, Ayrshire, in 1843. [NRS.AD14.43.375]

DEMPSTER, JOHN, a merchant from Greenock, died in Halifax, Nova Scotia, on 25 October 1848. [EEC.21743] [SG.1272]

DENNISON, JAMES, born 1755 in Culreach, a schoolmaster in Balmaghie, Kirkcudbrightshire, later in Virginia, died in Gatehouse of Fleet on 19 December 1824. [Anwoth gravestone, Kirkcudbrightshire]

DENNISTOUN, JAMES, son of James Dennistoun a merchant in Dumfries, was educated at Glasgow University, a minister in Jamaica from 1842 to 1847, in Constantinople, Turkey, from 1847 to 1848, in Malta from 1849 to 1851, and in Jamaica from 1851 until 1890. [F.7.669]

DENNISTON, ROBERT, born 7 August 1816, died in Toronto, Ontario, on 7 March 1853. [Whithorn gravestone, Wigtownshire]

DEWAR, DAVID BURTON, born 1796 at Castle Semple, died at Montego Bay, St James, Jamaica, on 31 July 1816. [Montego Bay gravestone]

DEWAR, PETER, with his wife and family, emigrated from Greenock to Quebec in July 1804, settled in St Andrews, Quebec. [CP]

DEWAR, WILLIAM, born on 15 March 1801 in Paisley, died at Montego Bay, St James, Jamaica, on 10 July 1858. [Montego Bay gravestone]

DICK, GILBERT, master of the Europe of Ayr from Greenock to Quebec in 1814. [NRS.E504.15.103]SG.1817]

DICKIE, ROBERT, a farmer late of Auld Mains of Kilwinning in Ayrshire, died in Beverly, Galt, Upper Canada, on 10 March 1849. [

DICKSON, DAVID, a machine maker in Hutchestown, Glasgow, son of John Dickson in Lockerbie, Dumfries-shire, heir to his grandfather David Dickson, postmaster of Lockerbie in 1839. [NRS.CS237.D9.45]

DICKSON, MARY, born 1830, daughter of David Dickson, a solicitor in Maxwelltown, Dumfries-shire, died in Jersey City, New Jersey, in 1856. [DGC.16.9.1856]

DICKSON, THOMAS, died in Queenstown, Upper Canada, on 22 January 1825; his relict Archange Grant, in Dumfries, testament, 28 April 1829. [NRS]

DICKSON, WILLIAM, born 1769 in Dumfries, emigrated to Canada in 1792, settled in Niagara, Upper Canada, a lawyer and a politician, died on 19 February 1846. [CP]

DILL, WILLIAM, messenger at arms in Newton Stewart, Wigtownshire, in 1849. [POD]

DINWIDDIE, JANE ISABELLA, born 1854, daughter of Robert Dinwiddie a merchant, died in New York on 10 August 1859. [AO]

DINWIDDIE, ROBERT, born 23 July 1811 in Dumfries, a banker in New York from 1835, died there on 12 July 1888. [ANY]

DINWIDDIE, WILLIAM, born 1841, a joiner, son of David Dinwiddie in Annan, Dumfries-shire, died in Jefferson Street, Brooklyn, New York, on 11 January 1873. [AO]

DOBIE, JAMES, agent of the Western Bank of Scotland in Beith, Ayrshire, in 1849. [POD]

DOBIE, JEAN, a victim of assault and robbery in High Street, Lockerbie, Dumfries-shire, in 1830. [NRS.AD14,30.146]

DOBIE, THOMAS, son of Mr Dobie a writer in Lockerbie, Dumfries-shire, died in Jamaica in 1803. [AJ.2930]

DOBIE, ..., master of the Hero of Dumfries trading with Ulverston in 1823, and master of the Hopetoun of Dumfries trading with Ulverston in 1826. [NRS.E504.9.10]

DOBSON, HENRY, born 1822, a ploughman to Alexander Livingston in Potterland, Kelton, Kirkcudbrightshire, was accused of forgery and theft in 1850. [NRS.A14.50.521]

DODD, FRANCIS DUNLOP, born 3 September 1818 in Ayrshire, Senior Magistrate in Hanover, Jamaica, died on 7 November 1891. [Green Island gravestone, Jamaica]

DODD, WILLIAM, a skipper in Greenock, testament, 1822, Comm. Glasgow. [NRS]

DOGHERTY, EDWARD, guilty of theft, was sentenced to 12 months in Ayr Tolbooth in 1820. [NRS.JC26.1820.129]

DOLLAR, WILLIAM, born 1797, a shoemaker in Greenock, emigrated via Port Glasgow aboard the Favourite of St John bound for St John, New Brunswick, on 22 October 1815. [PANB.ms.RS23E.9798]

DONALD, ANDREW, son of William Donald jr. a merchant in Greenock, settled in Bedford County, Virginia, by 1799. [NRS.RS81.19]

DONALD, ROBERT, formerly a merchant in Pensacola, Florida, later in Ayr, testament, 10 February 1791, Comm. Ayr. [NRS]

DONALDSON, ROBERT, born 4 March 1764 in Barnkiss, Dumfries-shire, son of John Donaldson and his wife Margaret Tait, a merchant in New York, died in Brunswick County, North Carolina, on 8 July 1808. [ANY]

DONALDSON, ROBERT, in Greenock, applied to settle in Canada on 4 March 1815. [NRS.RH9]

DONNAN, JOHN, born 1810, son of John and Jane Donnan in Culscadden, died in Pittsburgh, Pennsylvania, on 28 June 1838. [Whithorn gravestone, Wigtownshire]

DONOLLY, CHARLES, a victim of assault etc. at the Old Foundry, West Hawkhill farm, St Quivox, Ayrshire, in 1843. [NRS.AD14.43.375]

DOUGLAS, ADAM, born 1813, a nailer in Annan, Dumfries-shire, was accused of bigamy in 1842. [NRS.JC26.1842.280]

DOUGLAS, DANIEL, [1822-1890], father of William Douglas born 1864, died in Philadelphia, Pennsylvania, on 21 August 1888. [Stair gravestone, Ayrshire]

DOUGLAS, ELIZABETH, a widow in the Coal House, Mansion House, Orchardton, Kirkcudbrightshire, a victim of theft in 1824. [NRS.AD14.24.150]

DOUGLAS, GEORGE, born in Castle Douglas, Dumfries-shire, son of John Douglas and his wife Mary Heron, a merchant in New York, died in Peerskill, N.Y., on 9 October 1799. [ANY] Roxburghshire, emigrated to America in 1818. [UPC]

DOUGLAS, HUGH, born 1824, a stone dyker or farm servant in Dumfries, was accused of poaching in 1849. [NRS.AD14.49.232]

DOUGLAS, JAMES, born 1772 in Galloway, a mariner, applied to become a citizen of South Carolina on 10 December 1804. [NARA]

DOUGLAS, JAMES, sr., born 1770 in Dumfries-shire, died in Maitland Village, Nova Scotia, on 23 May 1843. [NSRG.8.6.1843]

DOUGLAS, JAMES, from Kirkcudbright, was educated at Theological Hall from 1808 to 1812, ordained in 1813, a minister in Chirnside, Roxburghshire, who emigrated to America 1818. [UPC]

DOUGLAS, JOHN, son of James Douglas the Provost of Gatehouse of Fleet, Kirkcudbrightshire, died in Kingston, Jamaica, in 1813. [AJ.3410]

DOUGLAS, JOHN, born 1780 in Dumfries-shire, a brewer, distiller, and storekeeper, settled in Whitestown, Oneida County, New York, was naturalised on 2 May 1821 and 11 October 1830 in N.Y. [NY Court of Common Pleas] [NY Superior Court]

DOUGLAS, JOHN, born 1796 in Castle Stewart, Wigtownshire, emigrated to America, died 2 November 1832, buried in Monacacy cemetery, Montgomery County, Maryland. [HGM]

DOUGLAS, JOSEPH, found guilty of theft and was sentenced at Dumfries to seven years transportation to the colonies in 1814. [NRS.GD1.959]

DOUGLAS, Reverend ROBERT, born 1781 in Roxburghshire emigrated to Nova Scotia in 1816, a minister in Nova Scotia and on Prince Edward Island from 1816 until his death on 17 September 1846. [HPC]

DOUGLAS, ROBERT, third son of Reverend James Douglas in Stewarton, Ayrshire, was educated at Glasgow University in 1813, a surgeon in Tobago. [MAGU]

DOUGLAS, ROBERT, MD, born 1814, son of William Douglas, [1785-1853], and his wife Janet Walker, [1788-1868], was educated at the University of Glasgow, a physician in New York, died at 10 Bleecker Street, N.Y. on 25 July 1861. [Johnstone gravestone, Renfrewshire] [S.1923]

DOUGLAS, SAMUEL, probably from Galloway, formerly in Savanna, Georgia, late in Jamaica, probate, April 1823, PCC. [TNA]

DOUGLAS, THOMAS DUNLOP, in Dunlop, born 1 January 1776, died 30 January 1869. [Dunlop gravestone, Ayrshire]

DOUGLAS, WILLIAM, master of the <u>Commerce of Ayr</u> trading with Dublin in 1818. [NRS.E504.4.14]

DOUGLAS, WILLIAM, on the <u>Draper of New York</u> from Castle Douglas, Kirkcudbrightshire, married Isabell Vivers, daughter of Captain John Vivers of the <u>Ann of Annan</u>, late of New Jersey, in Jersey City, N.J., on 20 July 1865. [AO]

DOWNIE, WILLIAM, born 1796, from Knockneen, Kirkcolm, Wigtownshire, died in Philadelphia, Pennsylvania, on 27 March 1847. [DGH.27.5.1847]

DRAFFIN, SAMUEL, born 1839, a labourer from Ayrshire, landed in Hobart, Tasmania, Australia, from the <u>Conway</u> on 14 October 1855. [SRA.TD292]

DRIPPS, MATTHEW, son of Matthew Dripps in Craigie, Ayrshire, was educated at Glasgow University in 1789, a missionary of the Secession Church in America, minister in Shelburne, Nova Scotia, died 1828. [MAGU]

DRUMMOND, WILLIAM, master of the <u>Amity of Ayr</u> trading with Dublin in 1818. [NRS.E504.4.14]

DUFF, Mrs HELEN, relict of Captain Duff from Kenziels, Annan, Dumfries-shire, died in New York on 25 February 1864. [AO]

DUFF, JANE, born 1837, daughter of James Duff and his wife Janet Kinnear, wife of Thomas McKnaught, died in New York on 18 October 1865. [Whithorn gravestone, Wigtownshire]

DUFF, MARY, from Dumfries-shire, married Andrew H. Rome a printer from Dumfriesshire, in Brooklyn, New York, on 6 April 1869. [AO]

DUNBAR, WILLIAM, in Xerris, Spain, was admitted as a burgess and guilds-brother of Ayr on 28 February 1791. [ABR]

DUNCAN, DONALD, son of James Duncan, died 1823, a merchant in Greenock, Renfrewshire, and Elizabeth Shaw, died 1806, died in St Louis on the River Mississippi. [Greenock gravestone]

DUNCAN, JAMES, a currier in New Jersey, son and heir of John Duncan a tanner in West Kilbride, Ayrshire, who died 4 April 1836. [NRS.S/H]

DUNCAN, JOHN, in Fairlie, Largs, Ayrshire, a victim of sheep thieves in 1837. [NRS.AD14.37.270]

DUNCAN, ROBERT, in Haplandmoor, born 1743, died 29 October 1816, husband of Jean Gemmill, born 1769, died 5 September 1826. [Dunlop gravestone, Ayrshire]

DUNLOP, JOHN, in Over Bordland, born 1740, died 27 January 1814, husband of Jean Gilmour, born 1747, died 28 November 1827. [Dunlop gravestone, Ayrshire]

DUNLOP, MARGARET, in Kingston, St Vincent, daughter and heir to her father John William Dunlop a shipmaster in Irvine, Ayrshire, 1851. [NRS.S/H]

DUNLOP, ROBERT GRAHAM, born 1790 in Greenock, son of Alexander Dunlop of Keppoch, died in Gairbraid, Goderich, Upper Canada, on 28 February 1841. [AJ.4868]

DUNLOP, ROBERT, eldest son of Patrick Dunlop of Alton Hill, Kilmarnock, Ayrshire, and Janet Lumsden Jopp, daughter of Robert Jopp the Government Paymaster, were married in Dunedin, New Zealand, on 3 May 1864. [AJ.6087]

DUNLOP, ROBERT, a merchant in Hamilton, Canada, son and heir of Jane Pennell, widow of Robert Dunlop a shipmaster in Greenock, Renfrewshire, who died 27 January 1865. [NRS.S/H]

DUNLOP, WILLIAM, a merchant from Greenock, in America by 1794. [NRS.CS17.1.13, 308]

DUNSMORE, JAMES, born 1805, coalmaster in Barleith, died 18 August 1832, husband of Elizabeth Hamilton, born 1804, died 13 August 1832. [Riccarton gravestone, Ayrshire]

DUNSMORE, ROBERT, born 1779, coalmaster in Hurlford, died 16 September 1835, husband of Jean Kirkland, born 1776, died 21 August 1832. [Riccarton gravestone, Ayrshire]

DYSON, DUNBAR SMITH, born 1806 in Kirkcudbrightshire, settled in New York by 1831, died in New Orleans, Louisiana, on 22 December 1848. [ANY]

DYSON, ROBERT, born 1790 in Galloway, son of James Dyson and his wife Margaret Smith, settled in New York by 1818, a merchant and financier, died in New Brunswick, New Jersey, on 31 October 1848. [ANY]

EAGLESHAM, WILLIAM, and his wife Margaret McGarva, parents of James Eaglesham, born 1859, died in Asheburton, New Zealand, on 16 December 1893. [Ballantrae gravestone, Ayrshire]

EARLE, MARY, wife of John Jardine an architect in New York, from Whithorn, Wigtownshire, died in East Chester, N.Y., on 19 May 1873. [EC.27663]

EDWARD, ANDREW, in Bridge of Weir, Renfrewshire, bound via Quebec to Upper Canada in 1820. [NRS.SC58.75.79]

ELLIOT, JOHN, a resident of George Street in the parish of St Quivox, Ayrshire, was admitted as a burgess and freeman of Ayr on 13 April 1831. [ABR]

EVANS, JOHN, a purser in the Royal Navy, spouse of Elizabeth Maxwell in Dumfries, testament, 1828, Comm. Dumfries. [NRS]

EWART, RICHARD J. W., born 1816 in Ruthwell, Dumfries-shire, brother of William Ewart a surgeon in Annan, settled in West Brighton, New York, in 1849, died on 23 April 1873. [AO]

EWART, ..., master of the Queensberry of Dumfries trading with Liverpool in 1825. [NRS.E504.9.10]

EWING, ELLEN, born 1822, wife of James Christie, died in Hastings, Canada, on 10 April 1887. [Galston gravestone, Ayrshire]

EWING, JAMES, a merchant in Greenock, a partner in the firm of Miller, Fergus, and Company, merchants in Newfoundland in 1823. [NRS.CS44.1824]

EWING, JOHN, a farmer and cattle-dealer in Newhouse, Largs, a sederunt book, 1832-1835. [NRS.CS96.4642]

EWING, ROBERT, born 1828, son of James Ewing, [1803-1854], a forester, died in Buffalo, New York, on 24 November 1893. [Galston gravestone, Ayrshire]

FAIRLIE, JAMES, a merchant in New York and in Virginia, then from 1783 to 1796 in Kingston, Jamaica, later in Kilmarnock. [NRS.NRAS.00396.TD248.2]

FAIRLIE, MARGARET, wife of Robert Fairlie from Greenock, died in Naperville, Du Page County, Illinois, on 11 September 1844. [SG.1342]

FARQUHAR, JOHN, a storekeeper, was admitted as a burgess and freeman of Ayr on 10 September 1800. [ABR]

FERGUSON, A., in Johnstone, Renfrewshire, applied to settle in Canada on 28 February 1815. [NRS.RH9]

FERGUSON, DAVID, a merchant and Customs Collector of Ayr, father of David Ferguson a merchant in Virginia, 1793-1795. [NRS.CS17.1.391; CS17.1.14/26]

FERGUSON, DOUGALD, a cooper from Greenock, in Georgia by 1801. [NRS.CS17.1.9/425]

FERGUSON, FRANCIS, born in Dunlop, Ayrshire, emigrated to Canada in 1826, settled in Bathurst, New Brunswick. [RCF]

FERGUSON, JAMES, eldest son of William Ferguson of Townhead a merchant in Dumfries, settled in America by 1799. [NRS.CS26.909.2; CS17.1.24/341]

FERGUSON, JAMES, son of Joseph Ferguson, a painter in Dumfries, and his wife Nichola Hair, died in Toronto, Ontario, on 1 July 1836. [Dumfries gravestone]

FERGUSON, JOHN, a cooper from Greenock, settled in Georgia by 1801. [NRS.CS17.1.19/425]

FERGUSON, JOHN, late from Demerara, was admitted as a burgess and guilds-brother of Ayr on 1 October 1802. [ABR]

FERGUSON, JOHN, born 1813 in Dunlop, Ayrshire, emigrated to Canada in 1826, settled in Bathurst, New Brunswick. [RCF]

FERGUSON, JOHN, agent in Kirkcudbright, for the Western Bank of Scotland in 1849. [POD]

FERGUSON, MARTIN PATERSON, born 16 June 1826, son of John Ferguson, a merchant in Kilmarnock, Ayrshire, and his wife Elizabeth Muir, a minister in Argentina from 1862, died 2 September 1906. [F.7.681]

FERGUSON, ROBERT, in Oldhall, husband of Agnes Logan, born 1783, died 7 March 1848. [Dunlop gravestone, Ayrshire]

FERGUSON, ROBERT, born in Dunlop, Ayrshire, emigrated to Canada in 1826, settled in Bathurst, New Brunswick. [RCF]

FERGUSON, THOMAS, born 12 September 1799 in Inch, Wigtownshire, son of Reverend Peter Ferguson and his wife Marion Murray, was educated at Glasgow University in 1817, a surgeon in St John, Antigua, died on 21 May 1845. [F.2.337][MAGU]

FERGUSON, WILLIAM JOHN, a labourer in Sallochan Glen, Ballantrae, Ayrshire, was accuse of bigamy in 1843. [NRS.AD14.43.158]

FERGUSON, Captain, master of the Cruikston Castle of Greenock from the River Clyde to Miramachi, New Brunswick, in 1835, and to Savannah, Georgia, and New York, in 1836, [GA]; master of the Marquess of Clydesdale, from the River Clyde bound for New York in 1850. [BSL.IX.23/28]

FERRIER, HUGH, in Aquadilla, Porto Rica, heir to his cousin Peter Cochrane in Clippen, Renfrewshire, 1836. [NRS.S/H]

FINDLAY, JAMES, agent in Paisley for the Bank of Scotland in 1849. [POD]

FINDLAY, JOHN, the King's boatman in Kirkcudbright, testament, 1808, Comm. Kirkcudbright. [NRS]

FINDLAY, JOHN, jr., in Chicago, Illinois, son and heir of Margaret Fraser, wife of John Findlay sr., on the Isle of Whithorn, Wigtownshire, who died on 12 September 1862. [NRS.S/H]

FISHER, JAMES, in Johnstone, Renfrewshire, applied to settle in Canada on 28 February 1815. [NRS.RH9]

FISHER, JOHN, a joiner in Kirkton, Dumfries-shire, and his daughter Ann Fisher, were victims of theft in 1830. [NRS.AD14.30.131]

FISHER, PETER, master of the Cruikston Castle of Greenock from Greenock to Miramachi, New Brunswick, in 1830, from Greenock to Chaleur Bay, NB, or Pictou, Nova Scotia, or Prince Edward Island in 1831, from Greenock to New York in 1832 and to N.Y. and Savannah, Georgia, in 1836. [GA]

FLECK, JOHN, a skipper n Kilwinning, Ayrshire, testament, 1820, Comm. Glasgow. [NRS]

FLEMING, Captain JOHN, born in Greenock, Renfrewshire, late in Jamaica, died in Halifax, Nova Scotia, on 11 August 1830. [AR.14.8.1830]

FLEMING, or STEVENSON, MARY, in Kilmarnock, Ayrshire, died 27 April 1842, mother of Gabriel Stevenson, a merchant in Hamburg, Germany, in 1850. [NRS.S/H]

FLETCHER, JAMES, a miner at Albion Mines, Nova Scotia, heir to his brother Joseph Fletcher a collier in Crookedholm, Kilmarnock, Ayrshire, who died 20 February 1860. [NRS.S/H]

FISHER, ALEXANDER, in Johnstone, Renfrewshire, a victim of crime in 1820. [NRS.AD14.20.3]

FOLDER, ROBERT, a mariner in Summergate, Annan, testament, 1818, Comm. Dumfries. [NRS]

FORREST, JOHN, born in Annan, Dumfries-shire, son of James Forrest and his wife Agnes......, died in Brooklyn, New York, on 18 February 1866. [AO]

FOREST, WILLIAM, born 1800 in Dumfries, died in Digby, Nova Scotia, on 20 November 1843. [NBC.9.12.1843]

FORREST, WILLIAM, in Greenock, James, brother and heir of James Forrest a minister in the USA who died 18 February 1855. [NRS.S/H]

FORSYTH, AMBROSE, born 1840, son of William Forsyth, [1797-1846], died in Jamaica on 28 February 1870. [St Michael's gravestone, Dumfries]

FORSYTH, JANET, from Dumfries-shire, married Andrew Little of Kingsclear parish, New Brunswick, in Harvey, N.B. on 19 October 1843. [The Loyalist, 26.10.1843]

FORSYTH, NATHANIEL, born 1769 in Smailholm Bank, Dumfries-shire, a minister in India from 1798 until his death on 11 February 1816. [Union Chapel gravestone, Dhurrumtollah, Calcutta]

FORSYTH, WILLIAM, born 1797, a planter in the West Indies, died in Ladyfield, Dumfries, on 29 November 1846. [St Michael's gravestone, Dumfries]

FORSYTH, Reverend, born in Ecclesfechan, Dumfries-shire, a minister in Cornwallis, Prince Edward Island, from 1800 to 1835, died there on 9 August 1840. [HPC]

FOSTER, JANET, in Barr, Ayrshire, guilty of concealing pregnancy, sentenced to 12 months in Ayr Tolbooth in 1820. [NRS.JC26.1820.129]

FOULDS, JAMES, born 1794, son of William Foulds, a surgeon in Jamaica, died in 1817. [Dalry gravestone, Ayrshire]

FOWLER, Dr REEVES, born in Paisley, Renfrewshire, the Health Officer for New Providence in the Bahamas, died in the Marine Hospital, Staten Island, New York, on 14 November 1809. [Bahamas Royal Gazette, 20.12.1809]

FRASER, JAMES, born 1759 in Greenock, Renfrewshire, died in Darien, Georgia, on 18 December 1828. [Georgia Republican, 29.12.1828]

FRAZER, JOHN, a cloth merchant from Glasgow, was admitted as a burgess and freeman of Ayr on 4 March 1829. [ABR]

FRASER, JOSEPH, born 1811, a labourer in Kirkmahoe, Dumfries-shire, accused of poaching in 1832. [NRS.AD14.32.81]

FRASER, THOMAS, son of Thomas Fraser a merchant in Kilbarchan, Renfrewshire, was educated at Glasgow University in 1809, a Relief Church minister in Dalkeith in 1833, later in Niagara, USA, and in Lanark, Canada, died in Montreal, Quebec, on 15 July 1884. [MAGU] [UPC]

FRASER, WILLIAM, son of James Fraser, a surgeon in Dumfries, and his wife Eliza Hoyle, emigrated to Jamaica in 1830, died in Spanish Town, Jamaica, in 1863. [St Michael's gravestone, Jamaica]

FULLARTON, ALEXANDER, born 1825, a sawyer in Ayrshire, landed in Hobart, Tasmania, Australia, from the Conway on 14 October 1855. [SRA.TD292]

FULLARTON, GEORGE, was heir to lands in Irvine, Ayrshire in 1845 which he disposed of to John Ferguson of Cairnbrock. [NRS.GD3.1.62.72/73]

FULLARTON, HENRY, born 131, son of A. Fullarton in Castle Douglas, Kirkcudbrightshire, died in Astoria, Long Island, New York, on 16 November 1857. [DGH.25.121857]

FULTON, JAMES, born in Paisley, Renfrewshire, died on The Protector on 21 September 1816. [RG.16.10.1816]

GAIRDNER, ALEXANDER, fourth son of Alexander Gairdner in Ayr, died in Tobago on 18 January 1849. [EEC.21781]

GAIRDNER, C. D., agent in Kilmarnock, Ayrshire, for the Union Bank of Scotland in 1849. [POD]

GAIRDNER, JOHN, an Anti-Burgher and a soap-boiler, was admitted as a burgess and guild-brother of Ayr on 21 September 1808. [ABR]

GALL, CHARLES, born 1786, son of John Gall, [1748-1805], emigrated to Australia in 1851, died at Ballater Cottage, Adelaide, South Australia, on 29 September 1877. [Glencairn gravestone, Dumfries-shire]

GALLAN, ALEXANDER, a mariner in Greenock, testament, 1816, Comm. Glasgow. [NRS]

GALLOWAY, GEORGE, born 1802 in Kirkcudbright, son of George Galloway, was educated at Edinburgh University, a minister in Warwick, Bermuda, from 1833 until his death on 12 March 1834. [F.7.660]

GALT, WILLIAM, born 1755, probably in Dundonald, Ayrshire, settled in Virginia in 1775, a Presbyterian and a merchant who died in Richmond, Va., on 26 March 1825. [RRW]

GANCHEN, JAMES, was, with others, accused of murder, mobbing, rioting, and assault with firearms at the Old Foundry, West Hawkhill farm, St Quivox, Ayrshire, in 1843. [NRS.AD14.43.375]

GARDINER, JAMES, master of the <u>Kent of Greenock</u> from Glasgow bound for Montreal in 1842, [GSP][GH]; from Greenock bound for Canada but was wrecked on the Seven Isles in 1842. [EEC][FJ]

GARDNER, GEORGE, son of George Gardner, [1804-1844], died in America on 4 January 1858. [Whithorn gravestone, Wigtownshire]

GARR, ANDREW, born 1745 in Auchincairn, Kirkcudbrightshire, emigrated to New York in 1784, a shipbuilder there, died in N.Y. on 12 April 1812. [ANY]

GARRET, ANDREW, born 1795, from Inch, Wigtownshire, died in New York on 19 March 1858. [DGH.7.5.1858]

GARRETT, JAMES, born 1797 in Inch, Galloway, son of Robert Garrett a farmer, was educated at Glasgow University, emigrated to Australia in 1828, a minister in Tasmania from 1830 until his death in 1874. [F.7.601]

GEBBIE, ALEXANDER, MD, in Lowville, New York, son and heir of Robert Gebbie a weaver in Darvel, Ayrshire, who died 4 June 1863. [NRS.S/H]

GEBBIE, FRANCIS, born 3 May 1831 in Galston, Ayrshire, son of James Gebbie, a farmer, and his wife Ellen Smith, was educated at Glasgow University, a minister in Argentina from 1857 until 1883, died in Edinburgh in 1918. [F.7.681]

GEBBIE, HUGH, born 1754, a farmer on Springhill, died 15 December 1826. [Riccarton gravestone, Ayrshire]

GEMMELL, ALEXANDER, a skipper in Greenock, testament, 1803, Comm. Glasgow. [NRS]

GEMMELL, HUGH MITCHELL CAMPBELL, born 1827, second son of Dr Gemmell of Whitehill, Ayrshire, died in Hammerdale, St Kilda, Melbourne, Victoria, Australia, on 12 January 1880. [S.11388]

GEMMELL, JAMES, a farmer in Aiket, born1792, died 11 September 1879, husband of Jean Gilmour, born 1796, died 10 June 1858. [Dunlop gravestone, Ayrshire]

GEMMILL, JOHN, in Holehouse, born 1730, died 1815, husband of Mary Dunlop, born 1745, died 1824. [Dunlop gravestone, Ayrshire]

GEMMELL, JOHN, in Templehouse, born 1760, died 18 June 1819. [Dunlop gravestone, Ayrshire]

GEMMELL, ROBERT, born 25 December 1813, died 12 November 1874, husband of Janet Howie, born 1820, died in Ivy Cottage, Caldwell, on 6 March 1920. [Dunlop gravestone, Ayrshire]

GIBB, HELEN, daughter of James Gibb, [1791-1874], and his wife Helen Cook, settled in Elmira, New York. [Wallacetown gravestone, Ayrshire]

GIBB, THOMAS, son of James Gibb, [1791-1874], and his wife Helen Cook, died in Jersey City, New Jersey. [Wallacetown gravestone, Ayrshire]

GIBB, WILLIAM, born in Troon, Ayrshire, a carpenter aboard the <u>Eliza of Irvine</u> was drowned at St John, New Brunswick, on 22 May 1840. [Gleaner.26.5.1840]

GIBSON, ANN M., from Dumfries, married Adam Richardson, in New York on 23 February 1849. [DGH.12.4.1849]

GIBSON, ARCHIBALD, born 1805, son of James Gibson a sergeant of the Dumfries Militia, died at 19 Street, 8th Avenue, New York, on 31 October 1841. [DGH.16.2.1841]

GIBSON, JAMES, born 1753 in Paisley, Renfrewshire, son of William Gibson a shoemaker, emigrated to America by 1790, an accountant and merchant in New York, died on 20 September 1816. [ANY]

GIBSON, JOHN, a merchant in Virginia, son and heir of Robert Gibson a messenger in Kilmarnock, Ayrshire, 1791. [NRS.S/H]; 1793, 1796, [NRS.CS17.1.12.253; CS17.1.15/180]

GIBSON, JOHN, agent in Glenluce, Wigtownshire, for the Western Bank of Scotland in 1849. [POD]

GIBSON, WILLIAM, from Moffat, Dumfries-shire, applied for citizenship of South Carolina on 2 January 1798. [NARA.M1183]

GIBSON, WILLIAM, an apprentice aboard the Mary of Greenock, testament, 1805, Comm. Glasgow. [NRS]

GIBSON, WILLIAM, born 1810, son of William Gibson, [1780-1868], and his wife Agnes Henry, [1780-1858], died in Illinois on 12 August 1828. [Buittle gravestone, Wigtownshire]

GIBSON, WILLIAM, was, with others, accused of murder, mobbing, rioting, and assault with firearms at the Old Foundry, West Hawkhill farm, St Quivox, Ayrshire, in 1843. [NRS.AD14.43.375]

GILFILLAN, GEORGE, messenger at arms, Ayr, 1849. [POD]

GILLAN, JOSEPH, born 1813, a packman in Maxwelltown, Troquier, Stewartry of Kirkcudbright, was accused of housebreaking, theft, and reset at Hall of Drumpark, Irongray, Kirkcudbrightshire, in 1832. [NRS.AD14.32.57]

GILLESPIE, CHARLES, born 1813, son of John Gillespie in Caerlaverock, Dumfries-shire, died in Jamaica on 11 September 1836. [Caerlaverock gravestone]

GILLESPIE, JAMES, born 1796 in Greenock, a shipmaster who died on 19 October 1827. [Kingston, Jamaica, gravestone]

GILLESPIE, JOHN, messenger at arms in Greenock in 1849. [PO]

GILLESPIE, ROBERT, born 30 December 1778, son of Reverend John Gillespie and his wife Dorothea McKean in Kells, Kirkcudbrightshire, a merchant in New York, died 20 September 1830. [F.2.12]

GILLESPIE, ..., master of the Henrietta of Dumfries trading with Ulverston in 1826. [NRS.E504.9.10]

GILLIES, JAMES, born 1826, son of Duncan Gillies and his wife Janet Sibbald in Paisley, died in the West Indies on 27 December 1852. [Woodside gravestone, Paisley]

GILLIES, JOHN, a skipper in Greenock, testament, 1803, Comm. Glasgow. [NRS]

GILMORE, JOHN MORTON, in Lancaster, Virginia, grandson and heir of William Gilmore a candle-maker in Kilmarnock, Ayrshire, 1794; also, to his father Robert Gilmore a merchant in Virginia, 1795. [NRS.S/H]

GILMOUR, JOHN, in Ramsay, Upper Canada, brother and heir of William Gilmour a merchant in Paisley, Renfrewshire, 1833. [NRS.S/H]

GLAISTER, ROBERT, born 1771 in Greenock, a shipmaster who died in Savanna, Georgia, on 8 October 1806. [Savanna Death Register]

GLASGOW, ROBERT, of Montgreenan, Ayrshire, a planter of Montgreenan and Sans Souci in St Vincent from 1784 until 1831; a deed in St Vincent on 16 May 1795. [NRS.RD3.300.272; GD1.584.1]

GLEN, ANDREW, from Lochwinnoch, Renfrewshire, emigrated to Canada in 1818, was ordained in Montreal, Quebec, on 14 July 1818, a minister at Riviere du Chene and later at Richmond. [HPC]

GLENN, DAVID, married Ann Boyle in Ayrshire on 25 February 1795, emigrated to America in 1819, settled in Vevay, Switzerland County, Indiana, died in 1822. [BAF]

GLENN, JAMES ANDERSON, born in Paisley, settled as a tobacco merchant in Petersburg, Virginia, before 1822. [UNC; Glenn pp]

GLEN, ROBERT, master of the Isabella of Stranraer from Greenock to Newfoundland in 1815, [NRS.E504.15.108]

GLENDINNING, THOMAS, born 1833, eldest son of Robert Glendinning, formerly a farm steward in Outertown, Warimanbie, Dumfries-shire, died in Jersey City, New Jersey, on 6 February 1871. [AO]

GLENN, DAVID, from Ayrshire, married Ann Boyle in 1795, emigrated to America in 1819, settled in Vevay, Switzerland County, Indiana, 1822. [BLG]

GOLDIE, JOHN, born 1748, a wright, died 5 June 1822, husband of Jean Findlay. [Riccarton gravestone, Ayrshire]

GOLDIE, WILLIAM, agent of the Commercial Bank of Scotland in Dumfries in 1849. [POD]

GOOD, JAMES, master of the Marion of Ayr trading with Dublin in 1818. [NRS.E504.4.14]

GOOD, W., messenger at arms in Newton Stewart, Wigtownshire, in 1849. [POD]

GORDON, ELIZABETH, from Dumfries, emigrated via Belfast aboard the Shannon bound for New York on 18 January 1816. [PI]

GORDON, GEORGE, born 1794, Lighthouse keeper, died 29 August 1878, husband of Mary Shennen, born 1801, died 22 July 1873. [Cairnryan gravestone, Wigtownshire]

GORDON, JAMES, son of Alexander Gordon and his wife Anna Stroyan in the Mains of Penningham, Wigtownshire, settled in Charleston, South Carolina, died there in 1817. [GC]

GORDON, JAMES, born 1815, son of James Gordon and his wife Mary Robertson, died in Newlands, Victoria, Australia, on 1 September 1871. [Glencairn gravestone, Dumfries-shire]

GORDON, JOHN, son of Nathaniel Gordon, [1778-1850], and his wife Janet Coutts, [1794-1879], settled in Ballarat, Australia. [Glencairn gravestone, Dumfries-shire]

GORDON, JOHN, from Dumfries, emigrated via Belfast on the Shannon bound for New York in 1816. [PI]

GORDON, JOHN, born 8 September 1839 in Twynholm, Kirkcudbrightshire, son of Reverend John Gordon and his wife Penelope Murdoch, settled in New Zealand as a merchant. [F.2.429]

GORDON, ROBERT, born 1780 in Galloway, died in Shelburne, Nova Scotia, in 1830. [AR.20.3.1830]

GORDON, ROBERT, of Craig, disposed of the lands of Craig and Corse in Balmaclellan, in the Stewartry of Kirkcudbright, to Robert Robertson of Prendeguest on 20 February 1815. [NRS.CS230.M11.22]

GORDON, ROBERT, born 17 November 1829 in Dumfries, son of William Gordon and his wife Sarah Walker, a merchant in New York from 1846 to 1884, died in England on 16 May 1918. [ANY]

GORDON, THOMAS, born in Dumfries, died in Quebec on 26 July 1832. [EEC.18859] [AJ.4422]

GORDON, Captain WILLIAM, from Greenock, died in Toronto, Ontario, on 31 July 1849. [SG.1851]

GOUDIE, ROBERT, messenger at arms, Ayr, 1849. [POD]

GOURLAY, ELIZABETH, wife of William Harvey in Canada, daughter and heir of Helen Sproat, wife of Peter Gourlay a weaver in Kirkcudbright, 1857. [NRS.S/H]

GOURLAY, PETER, in Kirkcudbright, later in Lochgilphead, Argyll, sister of Samuel Gourlay in Jamaica, 1851. [NRS.S/H]

GOVAN, JAMES, a glasscutter from Greenock, settled in Mobile, Alabama, died in September 1849. [Inventory, 1855, Edinburgh, NRS]

GOWAN, PETER, born 1797 in Galloway, a watchmaker in Charleston, South Carolina, was naturalised there on 5 July 1848. [NARA.M1183.1]

GRACIE, JAMES, son of James Gracie and his wife Jean Cowan, a Brevet Major of the 21st Infantry, was killed at the Battle of Baltimore, Maryland, on 13 September 1813. [St Michael's gravestone, Dumfries]

GRACIE, WILLIAM, a merchant in Dumfries, father of William Gracie a merchant in Petersburg, Virginia, who died in Glasgow on 25 April 1792. [GCr.104]

GRAHAM, JAMES, born 1798 in Dumfries-shire, married Isabella Glendenning, settled in Streetsville, Ontario, before 1830. [SG.30.2.71]

GRAHAM, JAMES, was, with others, accused of murder, mobbing, rioting, and assault with firearms at the Old Foundry, West Hawkhill farm, St Quivox, Ayrshire, in 1843. [NRS.AD14.43.375]

GRAHAM, JOHN, born 1804, Deputy Post-Master General of Bombay, India, died at Kandalla near Poona, on 24 May 1839, husband of Ellen S. Stanley, born 1802, died 3 July 1834. [Westerkirk gravestone, Dumfries-shire]

GRAHAM, JOHN, born 1777, son of Thomas Graham, a farmer, and his wife Christian Halliday, in Burnswark, Ecclesfechan, Dumfries-shire, emigrated to New York in 1792, a merchant there, married Ann McQueen in 1804, died in N.Y. on 18 January 1843. [ANY][NRS.CS17.1.40/313]

GRAHAM, JOHN, born 1793 in Dumfries-shire, a timber merchant who died in Liverpool, Kent County, New Brunswick, on 1 March 1831. [NBC.19.3.1831]

GRAHAM, ROBERT, born 1816, son of John Graham, [1774-1830], and his wife Mary MacFie, [1780-1853], died in Jamaica on 5 March 1836. [Greenock gravestone]

GRAHAM, ROBERT, born 1798 in Dinwoodie Green, Dumfries-shire, died in Chatham, New Brunswick, on 17 October 1831. [GNS.18.10.1831]

GRAHAM, SIMON, possibly from Dumfries, emigrated via Greenock aboard the Maria of New York bound for New York on 27 March 1795. [NRS.SC15.55.2]

GRAINGER, ELIZABETH, wife of Henry Johnson a banker in Canada West, daughter and heir of Margaret Stirrat, wife of Luke Grainger a tailor in Paisley, Renfrewshire, 1871. [NRS.S/H]

GRAY, ANDREW, of Craigs, Dumfries-shire, died in Trenton, New Jersey, on 22 September 1819. [EA.5838]

GRAY, JAMES, master of the <u>Favourite of Ayr</u> from Greenock to Quebec in 1818. [NRS.E504.15.120]

GRAY, JOHN, master of the <u>Lochnell of Ayr</u> trading with Dublin in 1818. [NRS.E504.4.14]

GRAY, Captain, master of the <u>Diana of Greenock</u> from the Clyde bound for Newfoundland in 1843 also in 1844. [EEC.20607][GSP.870]

GREENSHIELDS, JANET, second daughter of Thomas Greenshields in Kilmarnock, Ayrshire, married Andrew Houston Young, in Quebec on 12 January 1841. [GM.ns15.200]

GREGORY, MARY, born 19 December 1791 in Kilmarnock, Ayrshire, daughter of William Gregory, a merchant, and his wife Elizabeth Smith, died in Rosebank, Paterson, New Jersey, on 14 November 1880. [Kilmarnock OPR]

GREGORY, PETER MALLARD, born 1797, fourth son of William Gregory in Kilmarnock, Ayrshire, died in Alexandria, Virginia, on 12 March 1817. [SM.79.479] [S.1.16]

GREIG, JOHN, a grocer, was admitted as a burgess and freeman of Ayr on 10 September 1800. [ABR]

GREIG, MICHELLE, born 1791, widow of John Steedman, from Kilmarnock, Ayrshire, died in New York on 18 December 1878. [EC.299401]

GREY, HUGH, born 1797 in Kilmarnock, Ayrshire, formerly in Wallace, Nova Scotia, died in Texas in 1840. [NCSG.3.4.1840]

GRIERSON, MARY, in Queensberry Street, Dumfries, a victim of forgery and theft in 1850. [NRS.AD14,50.521]

GRIERSON, WALTER, of Chapelmount, Dumfries, father of Francis W. Grierson, MB, CM Edin., born 1861, died in Sydney, New South Wales, on 8 January 1885. [S.12953]

GRIEVES, ARCHIBALD, born 1818 in Dumfries, died at 150 Chambers Street, New York, on 7 July 1856. [DGC.29.7.1856]

GUILLILAND, DAVID, an Anti-Burgher and a tobacconist, was admitted as a burgess and guild-brother of Ayr on 23 October 1816. [ABR]

GUTHRIE, JOHN, master of the Sister Ann of Ayr trading with Dublin in 1818. [NRS.E504.4.14]

HAINING, THOMAS, a messenger at arms in Dumfries in 1849. [POD]

HAIR, GEORGE, born 1789, son of Ninian Hair, died in St Thomas, Jamaica, on 27 February 1812. [Dumfries gravestone]

HALL, JANET, daughter of Alexander Hall, married Andrew Arthur a shipbuilder in New York, in Paisley, Renfrewshire, on 28 March 1848. [SG.1740]

HALL, MATTHEW, master of the Friendship of Ayr trading with Dublin in 1818. [NRS.E504.4.14]

HALL, THOMAS PARK, born 1823, second son of Captain Alexander Hall in Greenock, was drowned off St John, Newfoundland, on 19 July 1848. [SG.1740]

HALL, WILLIAM, in Eaglesham, Renfrewshire, a sequestration petition, 1849. [NRS.CS279.1033]

HALLIDAY, GEORGE, a block-cutter in New York, nephew and heir of Charles Liddell a smith in Barrhead, Renfrewshire, 1857. [NRS.S/H]

HALLIDAY, JEAN, wife of Peter Hughes a merchant in Newton Stewart, Wigtownshire, sister and heir of David Halliday in Jamaica, 1819. [NRS.S/H]

HALLIDAY, ROBERT, a merchant from Dumfries, died in New York on 11 April 1840. [DGH.29.5.1840]

HAMILTON, A., a messenger at arms in Dumfries in 1849. [POD]

HAMILTON, ALEXANDER, in Canada West, brother and heir of James Hamilton in Galston, Ayrshire, 1859. [NRS.S/H]

HAMILTON, ELIZA, youngest daughter of Captain Hamilton in Troon, Ayrshire, formerly a merchant in Ayr, married John Montgomery from

Dalhousie, New Brunswick, in Troon on 6 February 1834. [SG.217] [AJ.4493]

HAMILTON, JOHN, master of the Pitt of Ayr from Greenock to Quebec in 1817. [NRS.E504.15.116]

HAMILTON, JOHN, in 6 West Campbell Street, Broomlands, Paisley, a former soldier of the 15th Regiment of Foot, applied to settle in Canada on 12 March 1827. [TNA.CO384.5.887]

HAMILTON, MARY, and Marion Hamilton, in Ardrossan, Ayrshire, heirs of James Hamilton of Holmhead in 1833. [NRS.CS228.B17.81]

HAMILTON, PETER, a weaver in Millestown, Paisley, applied to settle in Canada on 22 April 1827. [TNA.CO384.5.891]

HAMILTON, ROBERT, in Jamaica, son and heir of James Hamilton the Provost of Sanquhar, 1820. [NRS.S/H]

HAMILTON, WILLIAM, master of the Alexander of Stranraer from Greenock to Newfoundland in 1814. [NRS.E504.15.105]

HAMILTON, WILLIAM, who died in America or somewhere abroad on 20 October 1817, son of George Hamilton in Renfrew, testament, 1825. [NRS.CC8.8.150]

HAMILTON, WILLIAM, born 1836, died on 17 April 1867, buried in Chicago, Illinois. [Galston gravestone, Ayrshire]

HAMILTON, Captain, master of the Corsair of Greenock from the River Clyde to Prince Edward Island and Chaleur Bay, New Brunswick, in 1830. [GA.3141]

HANNAH, ANDREW, from Galloway, a merchant, applied to become a citizen of South Carolina on 9 November 1807. [NARA]

HANNAH, JAMES, master of the Europe of Ayr from Greenock to Miramachi, New Brunswick, in 1814; master of the Hazard of Ayr from Greenock bound for Philadelphia, Pennsylvania, in 1817 and 1818. [NRS.E504.15.105/116/119]

HANNAH, MARION, wife of A. McQueen a weaver in Wigtown, sister and heir to her brother Peter Hannah a merchant in Petersburg, Virginia, 1829. [NRS.S/H]

HANNAY, ALEXANDER, agent of the National Bank of Scotland in Dumfries in 1849. [POD]

HANNAY, JAMES, a mariner in Kirkcudbright, inventory, 1815, Comm. Kirkcudbright. [NRS]

HANNAY, MARGARET, in Newton Stewart, Dumfries-shire, sister and heir of Thomas MacKnaight in Grenada, 1827. [NRS.S/H]

HANNELL, PATRICK, a tenant in Caldens, Wigtownshire, who died in Virginia, testament, 1823. [NRS.CC8.8.149]

HARDGRAVE, FLORENCE, born 1849, youngest daughter of Alexander Hardgrave and his wife Mary Anne Bell from Ruthwell, Dumfries-shire, died in New York on 27 October 1864. [AO]

HARKNESS, ALEXANDER, formerly a teacher of the Free Middle School in Paisley, Renfrewshire, died in Philadelphia, Pennsylvania, on 6 October 1849. [SG.1870]

HARKNESS, JAMES, son of James Harkness a manufacturer in Sanquhar, Dumfries-shire, was educated at Glasgow University in 1800, later was minister of St Andrew's Presbyterian Church in Quebec in 1820. [MAGU]

HARKNESS, Mrs JANE, born 1770 in Dumfries, settled in New Brunswick in 1839, died in Tabisuntac, N.B., on 1 April 1841. [STA.27.4.1841]

HARKNESS, WALTER, born 1801, son of William Harkness, [1776-1848], a farmer, and his wife Elizabeth Corrie, a surgeon in Canada, who died on 3 January 1834. [Dumfries gravestone]

HARPER, JOHN, in Kilmaurs, Ayrshire, an employee of the Hudson Bay Company from 1818 until 1821. [HBRS]

HARPER, THOMAS, a wood merchant from Moniave, Dumfries-shire, settled in New York by 1855. [DGC.15.1.1856]

HARRIS, JEFFREY, in Richibucto, New Brunswick, son and heir of Jean Jeffrey, wife of J. Johnstone in Creetown, Kirkcudbrightshire, 1825. [NRS.S/H]

HARVEY, HENRY, master of the <u>Mary of Greenock</u>, married …. Parker, daughter of Captain Parker in St John, New Brunswick, there in November 1809. [DPCA.391]

HATHORN, Captain JOHN, of Castlewigg, owner of property in Rotten Row, Whithorn, Wigtownshire, between 1784 and 1863. [NRS.GD455.49]

HATTRICK, PETER, born 1755, a merchant from Greenock Renfrewshire, settled in New York by 1795, died there on 11 June 1832. [DGC.31.7.1832][NRS.RS.54.PR6.1231]

HAY, D., master of the <u>Columbia of Ardrossan</u> from the River Clyde bound for New York in 1850. [L]

HAY, FRANCIS, born 1773, died in Jamaica in 1811. [Dundonald gravestone, Ayrshire]

HAY, ROBERT, born 1841, from Nether Boreland, Dryfesdale, Dumfries-shire, died in New York on 25 November 1870. [AO]

HELME, WILLIAM, born 25 April 1824, emigrated to America as a child, a gas engineer in Trenton, New Jersey, later in Philadephia, Pennsylvania, died there on 12 June 1888. [AP]

HENDERSON, Captain ALEXANDER, from Greenock, Renfrewshire, died aboard the brig <u>H. N. Binney</u> en route from Jamaica to Halifax, Nova Scotia, on 27 December 1832. [HJ.21.1.1833]

HENDERSON, DAVID, born in Annan, Dumfries-shire, settled in New York by 1826, founder of the Arinondack Iron and Steel Company, died in Jersey City, New Jersey, on 3 September 1845. [DGH.2.10.1845][[ANY]

HENDERSON, JAMES, from Kilmacolm, Renfrewshire, was educated at Theology Hall in 1819, emigrated to America on 28 February 1821. [RPC]

HENDERSON, JOHN HALLY, son of Reverend John Henderson in Wanlockhead, Dumfries-shire, died in Jamaica on 3 October 1820. [F.3.329]

HENDERSON, THOMAS, born 1835 in Thornhill, Dumfries-shire, died in New York on 19 December 1862. [AO]

HENDRIE, JOHN, agent for the Union Bank of Scotland in Galston in 1849. [POD]

HENIE, Mrs JANE, born 1777 in Ayrshire, died in Georgia on 5 October 1815. [Georgia gravestone]

HENRY, JOHN, a joiner and cartwright in Chicago, Illinois, son and heir of John Henry a cabinetmaker in Greenock, Renfrewshire, who died on 1 October 1848. [NRS.S/H]

HENRY, MATTHEW, master of the Union of Greenock from Greenock to Quebec in 1815, 1820, 1821, also, to New Orleans, Louisiana, in 1816. [NRS.E504.15.109/111/128/131/135/139]

HERON, AGNES, born 1797 in Dumfries-shire, widow of James Savage, died at 328 South 2nd Street, New Jersey, on 4 July 1865. [AO]

HERON, PATRICK, born 4 December 1798, son of Reverend James Heron and his wife Mary Donaldson in Kirkgunzeon, Kirkcudbrightshire, died in St Kitts on 10 November 1824. [F.2.280] [Kirkgunzeon gravestone]

HERON, SAMUEL, born 1770 in Kirkcudbright, emigrated via New York to Canada, died in York, Upper Canada, in 1818. [DCB]

HERRIES, WILLIAM born 1778, son of John Herries and his wife Margaret Caven in Kirkgunzeon, Kirkcudbrightshire, died in Jamaica on 17 November 1805. [Kirkgunzeon gravestone]

HETHERINGTON, IRVING, born in Whaite, Ruthwell, Dumfries-shire, son of Richard Hederton and his wife Louisa Carruthers, was educated at Edinburgh University, emigrated to Australia on 24 March 1837, a minister in New South Wales and in Victoria, died on 5 July 1875. [F.7.590]

HETHERINGTON, MARY SCOTT, born 1794, widow of John Dixon, sister of Richard Hetherington in Searig, Dalton, Dumfries-shire, died in Preble, Cortland County, New York, on 0 September 1868. [AO]

HEUGHAN, CHARLES, born 1803, son of James Heughan, [1740-1802], and ……. Duff, [1740-1807], died in St John, New Brunswick, on 19 January 1832. [Buittle gravestone, Wigtownshire]

HILL, GEORGE MCCARTNEY, born 1780, son of George Hill of Blaiket, 1743-1810], and his wife Jean Callendar, a physician who died in St Croix, Danish West Indies, on 12 June 1824. [Dumfries gravestone]

HILL, Dr JAMES, born 1775, son of George Hill of Blaiket, [1743-1810], and Jean Callendar his wife, died in St Croix, Danish West Indies, on 11 June 1824. [BM.16.488][Dumfries gravestone]

HODGERT, JAMES, son of Rodger Hodgert a farmer in Johnstone, Renfrewshire, was educated at Glasgow University in 1814, died in Guelph, Ontario, on 19 November 1855. [MAGU]

HOGG, GEORGE, a merchant in Antigua, died in Paisley, Renfrewshire, on 28 February 1821. [EA]

HOGG, JOHN, son of James Hogg a draper in Dumfries, [1768-1833], and his wife Anne Stewart, died in New York aged 33. [Dumfries gravestone]

HOLIDAY, JANET, born 1813, from Raeburncleugh, Eskdale, Dumfries-shire, wife of Thomas Beattie from Ruthwell, Dumfries-shire, died in Truxton, Cortland, New York, on 4 June 1870. [AO]

HOLIDAY, WILLIAM, a planter at Goose Creek, South Carolina, cousin of Jean Bell at Nether Albie, Dumfries, probate, May 1810. [TNA]

HOLMES, JAMES, master of the <u>Greenfield of Irvine</u> from Greenock to Quebec in 1816, 1818. [NRS.E504.15.112/122/123]

HOLMES, JOHN, a surgeon from Paisley, Renfrewshire, died in Trinidad in 1804. [SM.66.973]

HOLMES, J., agent in Johnstone, Renfrewshire, for the Union Bank of Scotland in 1849. [POD]

HOLMES, ROBERT, born 1744 in Greenock, died in Falmouth, Jamaica, in 1807. [Jamaica gravestone]

HOLMES, SAMUEL, a skipper in Saltcoats, Ayrshire, testament, 1813, Comm. Glasgow. [NRS]

HOLMES, WILLIAM, master of the Jane Montgomerie of Irvine from Greenock to Quebec in 1817. [NRS.E504.15.116]

HOOD, JOHN, a merchant in Flower d'Hundred, Virginia, later in Greenock by 1802. [NRS.CS17.1.7; CS17.1.21/113]

HOOD, MATTHEW, born 1842, son of James Hood, [1802-1867], a cabinet maker, and his wife Margaret Crawford, [1802-1834], drowned at Detroit, Canada, [sic], on 11 September 1874. [St Andrews gravestone, Kilmarnock, Ayrshire]

HOPE, JAMES, a brewer in Annan, Dumfries-shire, sequestration, 1841. [NRS.CS280.27.43]

HOSSACK, JOHN, born 1756, of Glengaber and Buff Bay River, Jamaica, died on 19 October 1815. [Dumfries gravestone]

HOSSACK, MARY ANN, daughter of John Hossack of Buff Bay River Estate, Jamaica, and of Glencaber, Dumfries-shire, married John Bell of Woodstock, Custos Rotulorum at White River, St George, Jamaica, on 17 March 1828. [BM.24.404]

HOURIE, JOHN CHARLES, in Xerris, Spain, was admitted as a burgess and guilds-brother of Ayr on 28 February 1791. [ABR]

HOUSTON, ALEXANDER, a skipper in Greenock, testament, 1808, Comm. Glasgow. [NRS]

HOUSTON, ALEXANDER, in Largs, Ayrshire, was granted a licence for The Margaret in 1849. [NRS.CE7.1.4.17]

HOUSTON, JAMES, in 25 Queen Street, Paisley, a member of the Paisley Emigration Society, applied to settle in Canada on 26 September 1827. [TNA.CO384.5.897]

HOW, JOHN, master of the Friends of Saltcoats from Fort William, Inverness-shire, bound for Montreal, Quebec, in 1802. [GkAd.59]

HOWATSON, ANDREW SMITH, a storekeeper in Pittston, Pennsylvania, grandson and heir of Janet Cowan, widow of Andrew Smith in Longmyre, Kirkcudbrightshire, who died in 1825. [NRS.S/H]

HOWIE, JOHN, born 18 January 1833, died n Cambridge, Auckland, New Zealand, on 15 August 1868. [Fenwick gravestone, Ayrshire]

HOWIE, ROBERT, born 1802, died 2 June 1878, husband of Margaret McIndoe, born 1792, died 22 November 1878. [Dunlop gravestone, Ayrshire]

HOWIE, SAMUEL, in Greenock, Renfrewshire, later in Roscoe, North America, brother and heir of Isabella Howie, widow of John Alexander a feuar in Greenock, 1863. [NRS.S/H]

HUGHAN, THOMAS, of Airds, Dumfries-shire, married Lady Louisa Georgina Beauclerk, sister of the Duke of St Albans, in Munich, Germany, in 1836. [DPCA.1747]

HUIE, JAMES, the younger, a skipper from Dumfries in America in 1795. [NRS.CS17.1.14/123]

HUME, Reverend WILLIAM, born 1770 in Urr, Dumfries-shire, was educated at Edinburgh University, thirty years in Nashville, Tennessee, died there on 23 May 1833. [SG.156]

HUMPHREY, WILLIAM, jr., eldest son of .... Hunter a merchant in Greenock, Renfrewshire, died in Demerara in 1813. [EA.5174.13]

HUNTER, AGNES, from Dumfries, wife of Dr John Carson, died in Philadelphia, Pennsylvania, on 28 July 1826. [DGC.8.8.1826]

HUNTER, ANDREW HALLEY, in Newcastle, Canada West, son and heir of John Hunter, a teacher in Greenock, Renfrewshire, 1860. [NRS.S/H]

HUNTER, DAVID GILMORE, in Antis, Pennsylvania, son and heir of David Hunter a farmer in Thornyflat, Ayrshire, 1820. [NRS.S/H]

HUNTER, DAVID, and William Hunter, both labourers in Ellerslie, Kirkmahoe, Dumfries-shire, were accused of poaching in 1832. [NRS.AD14.32.81]

HUNTER, Reverend GEORGE PATTERSON, born 1838, son of Samuel Hunter and his wife Christina Gibson, died in New Zealand on 10 August 1928. [Dalry gravestone, Ayrshire]

HUNTER, HUGH, master of the Hercules of Ayr from Greenock to New Brunswick in 1818 and 1819. [NRS.E504.15.122/123/124]

HUNTER, JOHN, in America, third son of Mathew Hunter a mason in Galston, Ayrshire, 1808. [NRS.CS17.1.27/320]

HUNTER, JOHN, a master in the Royal Navy, later in Renfrew, testament, 1816, Comm. Hamilton. [NRS]

HUNTER, JOHN, a moulder in Canada, son and heir of Hugh Hunter in Newton on Ayr; also, to his uncle Charles Hunter, master of the Enterprise of Ayr, 1855. [NRS.S/H]

HUNTER, JOHN, born 1840, son of Samuel Hunter and his wife Christina Gibson, died in New Zealand on 19 July 1866. [Dalry gravestone, Ayrshire]

HUNTER, JOSEPH BLACK, born 1843, son of Samuel Hunter and his wife Christina Gibson, died in Hobart, Tasmania, on 27 April 1927. [Dalry gravestone, Ayrshire]

HUNTER, ROBERT, born 1759 in Galloway, emigrated via England to America, was naturalised in New York on 19 November 1804. [NYPL.ms]

HUNTER, SARAH, born 1846, son of Samuel Hunter and his wife Christina Gibson, died in Ida Valley, New Zealand, on 23 November 1931. [Dalry gravestone, Ayrshire]

HUNTER, THOMAS, in the Hall of Drumpark, Irongray, Kirkcudbrightshire, the victim of housebreakers, thieves and resetters in 1832. [NRS.AD14.32.57]

HUTCHINSON, ANDREW, born 1786 in Mauchline, Ayrshire, a carpenter who died in St John, New Brunswick, on 23 March 1831. [NBC.26.3.1831]

HUTCHISON, ALEXANDER, master of the Countess of Cassellis of Ayr trading with Belfast in 1818. [NRS.E504.4.14]

HUTCHISON, HUGH, in Morrison, Whiteside, Illinois, niece and heir of Reverend William Thomson in Old Monkland, Ayrshire, who died on 16 August 1841. [NRS.S/H]

HUTCHESON, JAMES, son of John Hutcheson of Fulbar, Renfrewshire, died on Burleigh Castle Estate, Tobago, in 1817. [S.42.17]

HUTCHISON, JANE, in Morrison, Whiteside, Illinois, nephew and heir of Reverend William Thomson in Old Monkland, Ayrshire, who died on 16 August 1841. [NRS.S/H]

HUTCHISON, JOHN, messenger at arms, Ayr, 1849. [POD]

HUTCHISON, ROBERT, in Morrison, Whiteside, Illinois, nephew and heir of Reverend William Thomson in Old Monkland, Ayrshire, who died on 16 August 1841. [NRS.S/H]

HUTCHISON, WILLIAM, son of Reverend Patrick Hutchison in Paisley, Renfrewshire, settled in New York in 1818, a merchant who died on 8 January 1875, testament, Edinburgh, 1875. [NRS][ANY]

HYDE, DAVID, and Company, merchants in Greenock, sederunt books, 1814-1835. [NRS.CS96.870]

HYSLOP, JEAN, daughter of William Hyslop of Lochend, Dumfries-shire, died in Jamaica on 9 November 1811, testament, Comm. Edinburgh, 1817. [NRS.CC8.8.143]

HYSLOP, MAXWELL, son of William Hyslop of Lochend, a merchant in New York, later in Kingston, Jamaica, by 1809. [NRS.CS17.1.28/400]; he married Mary Maxwell, second daughter of Wellwood Maxwell of Bancleugh in Dumfries on 29 October 1810. [DPCA.432]

HYSLOP, WELLWOOD, son of William Hyslop of Lochend, a merchant in New York, later in Kingston, Jamaica, by 1809. [NRS.CS17.1.28/400]; a merchant in New York in 1816. [NRS.CS17.1.35/168]; died in Kingston, Jamaica, on 16 February 1845. [Dumfries gravestone]

IMBRIE, JAMES, born 1780 in Paisley, Renfrewshire, son of Reverend James Imbrie and his wife Janet Pattison, a merchant who settled in Philadelphia, Pennsylvania, in 1805, died on 30 May 1835. [BLG]

INGLIS, SIMSON, son of Reverend Inglis in Dumfries, died in Tobago on 16 August 1802. [EA.4056.02]

IRVINE, ANDREW, from Dumfries-shire, was educated at Theological Hall from 1806 until 1809, emigrated to America in 1811. [RPC]

IRVINE, ….., master of the Nelly of Dumfries trading with Beaumaris in 1824. [NRS.E504.9.10]

IRVING, GEORGE, born 1769 in Dumfries-shire, was a butcher in St John, New Brunswick, for 10 years, died at Portland Bridge, N.B., on 5 September 1829. [NBC.12.9.1829]

IRVING, GEORGE, a mariner in Annan, Dumfries-shire, testament, 1825, Comm. Dumfries. [NRS]

IRVING, HELEN, born 1796 in Dumfries-shire, wife of Gilbert Dickson, died in Bovina, Delaware County, New York, on 11 April 1879. [AO]

IRVING, JAMES, born 1749 in Dumfries-shire, son of Dr James Irving, emigrated to the West Indies, Custos of Trelawney, Jamaica, died 21 November 1798. [Kingston gravestone, Jamaica]

IRVING, JAMES, a surgeon, lately in Jamaica, died in Gatehouse on 25 November 1821. [S.5.252]

IRVING, JAMES, born 1816, son of David Irving and Mary Broach in Kirkpatrick Fleming, Dumfries-shire, died in Trinidad on 4 February 1841. [Kirkpatrick Fleming gravestone]

IRVING, Mrs MARY, born 1795 in Dumfries-shire, wife of James Irving, died in Londonderry, Nova Scotia, on 16 May 1832. [HJ.2.7.1832]

IRVING, MARY, wife of Thomas Robertson a weaver in Ecclesfechan, Dumfries-shire, niece and heir of Walter Paisley in Jamaica, 1831. [NRS.S/H]

IRVING, PETER, in Kirktown, Dumfries-shire, master of the sloop Unity of Dumfries, inventory 1804, Comm. Dumfries. [NRS]

IRVING, WILLIAM, born 1790, son of James Irving and his wife Agnes Beattie in Caerlaverock, Dumfries-shire, died in Tobago on 2 January 1816. [Caerlaverock gravestone]

JACK, JOHN, a sloop-master in Largs, Ayrshire, testament, 1808, Comm. Glasgow. [NRS]

JACK, ROBERT, a machinist in Jersey City, New Jersey, son and heir of Robert Jack, a thread manufacturer in Paisley, Renfrewshire, who died 4 March 1860. [NRS.S/H]

JACKSON, ADAM, born 1791, son of Andrew Jackson in Annan, Dumfries-shire, died in Trinidad, on 25 January 1808. [Annan gravestone]

JACKSON, JOHN, in Shrewsbury, later in Hamilton, Ontario, son and heir of Edward Jackson in Paulsland, Dumfries-shire, who died 4 July 1845. [NRS.S/H]

JAFFRAY, JANE, born 29 May 1773, daughter of Reverend Andrew Jaffrey and his wife Agnes Armstrong in Ruthwell, Dumfries-shire, married ... Renwick in New York during 1794, died in 1850. [F.2.214]

JAFFREY, ROBERT, born 1779 in Kilmarnock, Ayrshire, son of Reverend Robert Jaffrey, was educated at Glasgow University around 1792, later a merchant in New York, heir to his father in 1825, died 11 June 1845. [ANY] [NRS.S/H]

JAFFREY, WILLIAM, the younger, an accountant in Campvale, Cathcart, Renfrewshire, trustee of John McKay an innkeeper in Airdrie, Lanarkshire, in 1827. [NRS.CS271.178]

JAMES, THOMAS, in Halifax, Nova Scotia, brother and heir of William James in Stranraer, Wigtownshire, who died 20 August 1843. [NRS.S/H]

JAMIESON, AGNES, in Largs, Ayrshire, petitioned re the inventory of John Jamieson in Ardeslat, Ayrshire, on 13 September 1810. [NRS.CC2.7.585]

JAMIESON, ARCHIBALD, and ELIZABETH JAMIESON in Ardinslat, Ayrshire, petitioned re the inventory of John Jamieson in Ardeslat, Ayrshire, on 13 September 1810. [NRS.CC2.7.585]

JAMIESON, JAMES, a brass founder in Greenock, son and heir of Christina Steel, widow of John Jamieson a surgeon, Charleston, America, who died on 10 September 1849. [NRS.S/H]

JAMIESON, JANET, in Indiana, grand-daughter and heir of Daniel Jamieson in Greenock who died in 1805. [NRS.S/H]

JAMIESON, JEAN, spouse of Hugh Reid a weaver in Largs, Ayrshire, petitioned re the inventory of John Jamieson in Ardeslat, Ayrshire, on 13 September 1810. [NRS.CC2.7.585]

JAMIESON, JOHN, from Kilmarnock, Ayrshire, and Eleanor Agnes Cook, daughter of John Cook in Halifax, Nova Scotia, were married in St John, New Brunswick, on 14 November 1825. [NBC.19.11.1825]

JAMIESON, JOHN, from Thornhill, Dumfries-shire, a minister in Bathgate from 1776 to 1783, emigrated to America, a minister in Pennsylvania from 1784 to 1797, died 1 July 1821. [UPC]

JAMIESON, NANCY LEE, wife of J. Stirrat in Baltimore, Maryland, heir to her grandfather Daniel Jamieson in Greenock, who died in 1805. [NRS.S/H]

JAMIESON, ROBERT, a skipper from Belfast, later in Greenock, testament, 1818, Comm. Glasgow. [NRS]

JAMIESON, ROBERT, son of Robert Jamieson of Castle Maddie, [1776-1838], in the Stewartry of Kirkcudbright, emigrated to Australia in 1837. [NRS.NRAS.775]

JAMIESON, THOMAS, in Largs, Ayrshire, petitioned re the inventory of John Jamieson in Ardeslat, Ayrshire, on 13 September 1810. [NRS.CC2.7.585]

JAMIESON, WILLIAM, son of Robert Jamieson of Castle Maddie, [1776-1838], in the Stewartry of Kirkcudbright, emigrated to Australia in 1840. [NRS.NRAS.775]

JAMIESON, WILLIAM, from Ayrshire, married Marion Lawrence, in Halifax, Nova Scotia, on 1 June 1842. [AR.4.6.1842]

JARDINE, ANDREW, born 1850, son of John Jardine of Rigg, Gretna, Dumfries-shire, settled in Rochelle, New York, died 19 February 1875. [AO]

JARDINE, ROBERT, from Dumfries-shire, and Gloranah Reed, daughter of Benjamin Reed, were married in Kingsclear, New Brunswick, on 8 December 1819. [NBRG.14.12.1819]

JARDINE, THOMAS, born 1808 in Lochmaben, Dumfries-shire, died in Pelham, West Chester, New York, on 13 January 1863. [AO]

JARDINE, WILLIAM, from Dumfries, a surgeon in the Royal Navy, testament, 1823, Comm. Dumfries. [NRS]

JARVIS, GEORGE, from Dumfries, a surgeon in the Royal Navy, testament, 1811, Comm. Hamilton. [NRS]

JEFFREY, JOHN, former minister of the Reformed Church in Quarelwood, Kirkmahoe, Dumfries-shire, died in New York on 25 December 1831. [AJ.4387]

JELLY, WILLIAM, a cartwright from Twynholm Kirk in the Stewartry of Kirkcudbright, died in November 1813 in Salem, Massachusetts, testament, 1821, [NRS.CC8.8.147]

JOHNSON, Mrs SARAH ELIZABETH, wife of W. Johnson the Attorney General of Prince Edward Island, died in Annan, Dumfries-shire, in 1824. [AR.1.5.1824]

JOHNSTON, ALEXANDER, a seaman in Greenock, testament, 1818, Comm. Glasgow. [NRS]

JOHNSTON, ALEXANDER, born 14 June 1810 at Barnboard Mill, Balmaghie, Kirkcudbrightshire, son of John Johnston and his wife

Margaret Rae, emigrated to South Carolina in 1835, later moved to New York, died in Scotland on 13 December 1845. [ANY]

JOHNSTONE, EBENEZER WILLIAM, second son of Reverend Thomas Johnstone in Dalry, Ayrshire, died in Skeldon, Upper Canada, on 26 August 1839. [SG.809]

JOHNSTON, EDWARD, in Girvan, Ayrshire, was accused of mobbing and rioting in 1817. [NRS.JC26.1817.225]

HUTCHISON, JOHN, messenger at arms, Ayr, 1849. [POD]

JOHNSTON, ALEXANDER, messenger at arms, Ayr, 1849. [POD]

JOHNSTON, ARCHIBALD SIMPSON, eldest son of Adam Johnston the Customs Collector in Greenock, Renfrewshire, died in Roslin, South Carolina, on 15 September 1819. [S.149.19]

JOHNSTON, ARCHIBALD, born 1798 in Dumfries-shire, a resident of Charleston, South Carolina, was admitted as a citizen of S.C. on 12 December 1825. [NARA.M1183.1]

JOHNSTON, ARCHIBALD, a builder in Glasgow, also contractor for the public buildings in Ayr was admitted as a burgess and freeman of Ayr on 9 April 1828. [ABR]

JOHNSTON, ELIZABETH, wife of W. Anderson on Prince Edward Island, sister and heir of John Johnstone in Annan, Dumfries-shire, 1854. [NRS.S/H]

JOHNSTON, ESTHER, wife of Theodore Wiepert in New York, her and grand-daughter of Douglas Johnstone a joiner in Annan, Dumfries-shire, who died 13 March 1858. [NRS.S/H]

JOHNSTON, FRANK, born 1827, eldest son of George Johnston of Newington Lodge, Annan, Dumfries-shire, died in New York on 15 June 1857. [AO]

JOHNSTON, GEORGE, born 1782 in Kirkcudbrightshire, son of William Johnston, settled in New York by 1804. [ANY][DGA.GGD.92/1]

JOHNSTON, GEORGE MILLIGAN, of Corehead, MD, a member of the American Philosophical Society, a Loyalist in Charleston, South Carolina, former Surgeon General to the British garrison in Georgia and South Carolina, died in Dumfries on 9 March 1799. [EA.3674.174] [TNA.AO.12.50.239, etc]

JOHNSTON, JAMES, son of William Johnson, [1778-1801], and his wife Jessie Thomson, [1773-1830], in Lockerbie, Dumfries-shire, died in St Lucia. [Dryfesdale gravestone, Dumfries-shire]

JOHNSTON, JAMES, a Lieutenant on HMS Bellerophon, inventory, 1810, Comm. Dumfries. [NRS]

JOHNSTON, JANET, daughter of John Johnston in Newton Closeburn, Dumfries-shire, married John Beck a merchant in New York on 4 January 1853, died in May 1882. [ANY]

JOHNSTON, JEFFREY, in Richibucto, New Brunswick, son and heir of Jean Johnston, wife of J. Johnstone in Creetown, Dumfries-shire, in 1825. [NRS.S/H]

JOHNSTON, JOHN, [1750-1841], miller at the Haugh of Urr, Kirkcudbrightshire, and his wife Dorothea Proudfoot, [1758-1794], parents of John Johnston, born 22 January 1781, who emigrated to New York in 1804 and died in Patterson, New Jersey, on 13 December 1846. [Balmaghie gravestone, Kirkcudbrightshire] [HOJ]

JOHNSTON, JOSEPH, in Lockerbie, Dumfries-shire, grandson and heir of Mary Stewart or Thomson in Annan, Dumfries-shire, 1837. [NRS.S/H]

JOHNSTON, MARGARET, of the Spur Inn, Loreburn Street, Dumfries, was a victim of forgery and theft in 1850. [NRS.AD14.50.521]

JOHNSTON, MARY, daughter of Robert Johnston a joiner in Ruthwell, Dumfries-shire, wife of Walter Burton from Ruthwell, died in Jersey City, New Jersey, on 3 August 1863. [AO]

JOHNSTONE, QUINTIN, a writer, was admitted as a burgess and guilds-brother of Ayr on 24 September 1800. [ABR]

JOHNSTONE, QUINTIN, in Chicago, Illinois, son and heir of Quintin Johnston of Trolorg, a writer in Ayrshire, who died on 21 November 1869. [NRS.S/H]

JOHNSTON, ROBERT, born 1804 in Kirkcudbrightshire, emigrated via Liverpool to America, an accountant who was naturalised in New York on 29 October 1821. [NY Court of Common Pleas][ANY]

JOHNSTONE, THOMAS, born 11 January 1829 in Garrell, Dumfries-shire, son of William Johnstone and his wife Elizabeth Renwick, was educated at the University of St Andrews, emigrated to Australia in 1856, a minister in New South Wales from 1856 to 1903, died on 3 February 1909. [F.7.590]

JOHNSTON, WILLIAM, born 1800 in Kirkcudbrightshire, emigrated via Greenock to America, a merchant who was naturalised in New York on 27 October 1821. [NY Court of Common Pleas]

JOHNSTON, WILLIAM, born 1803, son of John Johnston, [1766-1836], died on St Bartholemew, French West Indies, on 21 November 1827. [Dumfries gravestone]

JOHNSTON, WILLIAM, married Margaret Thomson in Canonbie, Dumfries-shire, on 24 April 1811, settled in Ontario by 1830. [SG.32.2.63]

JOHNSTON, ..., brother of John Johnston, a spirit dealer in Dumfries, settled in New York in 1807. [NRS.CS235.SB.J2]

JORIE, ALEXANDER, born 1801, son of John Jorie a merchant in Whithorn, died in Demerara on 1 August 1819. [Whithorn gravestone, Wigtownshire]

JORIE, JOHN, in Whithorn, Wigtownshire, the victim of an assault in 1837. [NRS.AD14.37.218]

KAY, JOHN, a merchant in Montreal, Quebec, brother and heir of Robert Kay a writer in Kilmarnock, Ayrshire, 1853. [NRS.S/H]

KEIR, ALEXANDER, from Newton Stewart, Wigtownshire, emigrated via Londonderry aboard the Barkley on 14 August 1816. [NWI.2.3

KENNEDY, ALEXANDER, born 1795 in Kelton, Kirkcudbrightshire, an overseer on the Hopewell Estate, Trelawney, Jamaica, died on 19 January 1832. [Falmouth gravestone, Jamaica]

KENNEDY, DANIEL, an Anti-Burgher and an innkeeper, was admitted as a burgess and guild-brother of Ayr on 23 October 1819. [ABR]

KENNEDY, DAVID, born in Ayrshire, a carpenter who died in Fredericton, New Brunswick, in December 1804. [NBRG.5.12.1804]

KENNEDY, DAVID SPROAT, born 1791 in Kirkcudbright, son of Captain John Kennedy and his wife Mary Lenox, a merchant in New York from 1807 to 1825. [ANY]

KENNEDY, GEORGE, in Cherry Villa, Ontario, heir to his great great grandfather Daniel Shaw, a weaver in Maxwellton, Paisley, Renfrewshire, who died in 1837. [NRS.S/H]

KENNEDY, JAMES LENOX, born in Kirkcudbright, son of Captain John Kennedy and his wife Mary Lenox, arrived in Glenthorn in 1815, a merchant in New York in 1818, later a merchant and US Consul in Mazatlan, Mexico, died there in 1838. [NRS.CS17.1.38/195][ANY]

KENNEDY, JOHN, from Kirkcudbright, died on his passage home from New York on 5 January 1797. [GM.67.165]

KENNEDY, JOHN, a skipper in Portpatrick, Wigtownshire, inventory, 1801, Comm. Wigtown. [NRS]

KENT, Mrs JANET, born 1822, daughter of Marion Scott from Annan, Dumfries-shire, died in West Philadelphia on 27 August 1857. [AO]

KERR, CHARLES, master of the Fame of Ayr trading with Dublin in 1818. [NRS.E504.4.14]

KERR, EDWARD, youngest grandson of Edward Kerr a merchant in Irvine, in Virginia by 1798. [NRS.CS17.1.17/59]

KERR, ELIZA, second daughter of William Kerr a merchant from Paisley, married Donald Mackay a merchant, in Montreal,F Quebec, on 30 July 1833. [SG.177]

KERR, GEORGE BROWN, in Newcastle, Hanover, Virginia, son of John Cunningham youngest brother of Sir William Cunningham Fairlie of Robertland and Fairlie in 1813; a merchant in Norfolk, Virginia, in 1820. [NRS.CS17.1.34/362; CS17.1.39/491]

KERR, JAMES, born 1754, a Captain of the Queen's Rangers during the American War of Independence, died in Amherst, Nova Scotia, on 6 June 1830. [NBRG.23.6.1830]

KERR, JOHN, master of the Industry of Stranraer trading with Larne in 1820. [NRS.E504.29.17]

KERR, JOHN, born 29 August 1815 in Dalry, Ayrshire, son of Hugh Kerr and his wife Jane Boyle, emigrated to America in 1841, settled as a joiner and farmer in Paddock's Grove, Maddison County, Illinois, returned to Dalry in 1853. [NLS letter]

KERR, ROBERT, born 1773, surgeon of the 21st Light Dragoon Regiment, died on 20 June 1803, buried in Clonmell, Ireland. [Riccarton gravestone, Ayrshire]

KERR, Dr THOMAS, born 1781, son of John Kerr and his wife Janet Irving in Lochmaben, Dumfries-shire, died in Jamaica on 12 August 1803 [Lochmaben gravestone]

KERR, WILLIAM, in Manchester, Virginia, later in Beith, Ayrshire, testament, Glasgow, 1813. [NRS]

KEVAN, ANDREW, born 1757 in Kirkcudbright, a shoemaker in New York, married Jean Dill on 22 June 1806, died there on 26 April 1827. [ANY]

KEVAN, SAMUEL, born in Kirkcudbrightshire, a master slater in New York by 1827, married Mary Tannahill in Schenectady, N.Y. in 1831. [ANY]

KEVAN, WILLIAM, born 1765 in Kirkcudbright, a leather and shoe merchant in New York before 1808, died there on 7 December 1847. [ANY]

KILPATRICK, JOHN DAVID, born 1805 in Dumfries-shire, died in St John, New Brunswick, on 7 May 1833. [NBC.7.5.1833]

KING, AGNES, from Paisley, Renfrewshire, later in South Carolina, niece and heir of John King in New York, 1820. [NRS.S/H]

KING, ALEXANDER, son of John King, a builder in Houston, Renfrewshire, and his wife Mary Barr, died in St Vincent on 23 March 1864. [Houston gravestone]

KING, CHARLES, born 1800 in Dumfries-shire, a slater with his wife Mary born 1798 in Galloway, and daughter Mary born 1825 in Dumfries, emigrated via Port Patrick and Belfast to America, were naturalised in New York on 20 October 1826. [NY Court of Common Pleas]

KING, SARAH, from Paisley, settled in South Carolina, niece and heir of John King in New York, 1820. [NRS.S/H]

KING, WARDEN, son of John King, [died 1844], and his wife Margaret Warden, [died in December 1823], settled in Montreal, Quebec. [Gourock gravestone, Renfrewshire]

KING, WILLIAM, a distiller in Largs, Ayrshire, sederunt book, 1831-1832. [NRS.CS96.2084]

KING, WILLIAM, agent of the Commercial Bank of Scotland in Beith, Ayrshire, in 1849. [POD]

KINNAN, ROBERT, a skipper in Greenock, testament, 1823, Comm. Glasgow. [NRS]

KIRK, ADAM, son of John Kirk a shoemaker in Kilmarnock, Ayrshire, settled in St George, Grenada before 1811, dead by March 1817. [NRS.GD1.632.1/12]

KIRK, GEORGE, in Inverwell, Sorbie, Wigtownshire, the victim of an assault in 1837. [NRS.AD14.37.218]

KIRK, Captain JOSEPH, master of the <u>Nancy of Dumfries</u> died at L'Etang, Charlotte County, New Brunswick, on 21 June 1824. [NBC.3.7.1824]; testament, 1825, Comm. Dumfries. [NRS]

KIRK, THOMAS, in St John, Antigua, nephew and heir of Andrew Kirk in Gatehouse, Kirkcudbrightshire, died 9 June 1865. [NRS.S/H]

KIRKPATRICK, JOHN, in Smithholm, Tinwald, testament, 1797, Comm. Dumfries. [NRS]

KIRKPATRICK, JOHN, born 1779 in Galloway, a merchant, was admitted as a citizen of South Carolina on 8 August 1805. [NARA.M1183.1]

KIRKPATRICK, JOSEPH, in Nether Keir, testament, 1792, Comm. Dumfries. [NRS]

KIRKPATRICK, ROBERT, in Haggs of Colin, testament, 1792, Comm. Dumfries. [NRS]

KIRKPATRICK, THOMAS, in Kingston, Jamaica, son and heir of Watson Kirkpatrick of High Kelton, Dumfries-shire, in 1828. [NRS.S/H]

KIRKPATRICK, WILLIAM, a merchant and baillie of Dumfries, testament, 1793, Comm. Dumfries. [NRS]

KIRKWOOD, ALEXANDER, a watch and clock-maker in Paisley, Renfrewshire, was admitted as a burgess and guilds-brother of Glasgow, on 10 September 1817, by right of his wife Elizabeth McKechnie, daughter of John McKechnie a burgess and guilds-brother. [GBR]

KIRKWOOD, DAVID, in Lochbridgehills, born 1784, died 27 August 1846, husband of Margaret Stevenson, born 1793, died 14 November 1864. [Dunlop gravestone, Ayrshire]

KIRKWOOD, ROBERT, from Paisley, Renfrewshire, a divinity student in 1823, later a minister in America. [AUPC]

KIRKWOOD, WILLIAM, born 1786, a merchant from Girvan, Ayrshire, emigrated via Greenock on the <u>William of New York</u> on 4 September 1817 bound for New York, arrived there on 17 October 1817. [NY Municipal Archives] [NY Commercial Advertiser, 18.10.1817]

KNOX, ALEXANDER, born 1788 in Paisley, Renfrewshire, son of Alexander Knox a weaver, died in Jane Street, New York, on 22 December 1851. [ANY]

KNOX, Mrs MARY, a widow, born 1769 in Paisley, Renfrewshire, was naturalised in New York on 22 December 1830. [NY Court of Common Pleas]

KNOX, ROBERT DADE, in Wilkes County, Georgia, great grandson and heir of John Knox a ship's carpenter in Renfrew, 1820. [NRS.S/H]; a deed in 1829. [NRS.RD5.398.456]

KNUTTON, Mrs MARGARET, possibly from Paisley, Renfrewshire, a widow in St John, New Brunswick, probate 1829, N.B.

KYLE, MATTHEW, in Tobago, son and heir of Andrew Kyle a farmer in Crookston, Renfrewshire, 1813. [NRS.S/H]

LACHLISON, ROBERT, in Burnside of Dunscore, testament, 1800, Comm. Dumfries. [NRS]

LAIDLAW, GEORGE, in Hightae, testament, 1793, Comm. Dumfries. [NRS]

LAING, WILLIAM, born in Greenock, a merchant in Tobago, died in Grenada on 14 July 1820. [S.4.192]

LAIRD, HUGH, a grocer in Crawfordykes, father of Andrew Laird a baker from Greenock, who settled in America by 1818. [NRS.CS17.1.38/29]

LAMB, Sir CHARLES, tacks of property in Old Ardrossan, Ayrshire, 1800-1836. [NRS.GD3.3.19]

LAMB, JEAN, in Ecclefechan, widow of ..... Dalgleish, testament, 1792, Comm. Dumfries. [NRS]

LAMBIE, JAMES, son of James Lambie, a farmer in Tarbolton, Ayrshire, was educated at Glasgow University in 1818, a minister in Pickering, and Whitby, Toronto, Ontario. [MAGU]

LAMONT, ALEXANDER, born 1756, a merchant in Kilmarnock, Ayrshire, died 3 August 1833, husband of Margaret Aitken, born 1759, died 17 February 1801. [Riccarton gravestone, Ayrshire]

LAMONT, COLIN DANIEL, a bank accountant in Greenock, nephew and heir of Duncan Lamont a merchant in New York who died 13 February 1865. [NRS.S/H]

LAMONT, DUNCAN, born 31 October 1792 in Greenock, Renfrewshire, a merchant in New York, died in Brooklyn, N.Y., on 13 February 1865. [ANY]

LAMONT, JOHN, a mariner in Crawforddykes, testament, 1807, Comm. Glasgow. [NRS]

LAMONT, JOHN, born 27 December 1805 in Kirkpatrick Durham, Dumfries-shire, son of Reverend David Lamont and his wife Anne Anderson, an advocate and later a brewer in London, died in Wangaratta, Victoria, Australia, in July 1873. [F.2.285]

LANG, Reverend GAVIN, minister of the Scots Church in Shelburne, Nova Scotia, married Ann Robertson Marshall, daughter of John Marshall, in Neilston, Renfrewshire, on 14 July 1829. [NBC.24.10.1829]

LANG, H. M., agent in Largs, Ayrshire, for the City of Glasgow Bank in 1849. [POD]

LANG, JAMES, agent in Largs, Ayrshire, for the Western Bank in 1849. [POD]

LAURIE, Sir ROBERT, of Maxwelltown, testament, 1791, Comm. Dumfries. [NRS]

LAW, ARCHIBALD, a skipper in Greenock, testament, 1814, Comm. Glasgow. [NRS]

LAWRIE, WILLIAM KENNEDY, of Redcastle, Galloway, born 1749, late of Woodhill Estate, St Thomas-in-the-East, Jamaica, died on 28 January 1811. [Bath Abbey gravestone]

LAWSON, JOHN, an innkeeper, was admitted as a burgess and freeman of Ayr on 12 May 1846. [ABR]

LAWSON, JOHN, the Inspector of the Poor in Annan, Dumfries-shire, in 1847. [NRS.CS244.813]

LAWSON, MARY, relict of Walter Owens an innkeeper in Dumfries, testament, 1799, Comm. Dumfries. [NRS]

LEARMONT, JOHN, with his wife Janet Jardine, and son John, emigrated from Dumfries-shire to Tobago in 1820. [Car.2.351]

LECKIE, JOHN MCRITCHIE, born 26 January 1851 in Parton, Dumfries-shire, son of Reverend Thomas Leckie and his wife Katherine McRitchie, was a sheep farmer in Australia. [F.2.422]

LEE, ALLAN, born 1777 in Paisley, Renfrewshire, a gardener who emigrated via Greenock to America, was naturalised in New York on 18 February 1817. [NY Court of Common Pleas]

LEECH, WILLIAM, third son of John Leech minister of the Secesssion Church in Largs, Ayrshire, died in Vernon, Mississippi, in 1831. [AJ.4384]

LEES, EDWARD S, from Dublin, Ireland, was admitted as a burgess and guilds-brother of Ayr on 29 April 1801. [ABR]

LEES, JOHN, in Dublin, Ireland, was admitted as a burgess and guilds-brother of Ayr on 29 April 1801. [ABR]

LEITCH, THOMAS, born 1836, a cutler from Renfrew, landed in Hobart, Tasmania, Australia, from the Conway on 14 October 1855. [SRA.TD292]

LENNOX, DAVID, son of James Lennox in Kirkcudbright, now in Philadelphia, Pennsylvania, was granted the lands of Port Mary on 2 February 1800. [NRS.RGS.131/118]

ENNOX, ROBERT, from Port Mary, Renwick, Stewartry of Kirkcudbright, a merchant in New York before 1829, a deed[NRS.RD5.387.745] LEYBURN, ROBERT, master of the Esther of Ayr from Greenock to Halifax, Nova Scotia, in 1814. [NRS.E504.15.103]

LIDDERDALE, JAMES, agent of the National Bank of Scotland in Castle Douglas, Dumfries-shire, in 1849. [POD]

LIGHTBODY, ISOBEL, in Dumfries, widow of John Hyslop in Boat of Dalswinton, sometime of Castlehill, testament 1793, Comm. Dumfries. [NRS]

LIMOND, ROBERT, son of David Limond an innkeeper burgess and guilds-brother of Ayr, formerly a Lieutenant Colonel in the Service of the East India Company, was admitted as a burgess and guilds-brother of Ayr on 24 September 1802. [ABR]

LINDSAY, ALEXANDER, MD, from Pinkieburn, Musselburgh, was admitted as a burgess and guilds-brother of Ayr on 10 September 1800. [ABR]

LINDSAY, ARCHIBALD, formerly in Clachan of New Abbey, later in Hydewood, testament 1796, Comm. Dumfries. [NRS]

LINTON, Dr DAVID, in St George, Grenada, later in Ayr, testament, 11 July 1809, Comm. Glasgow. [NRS]

LITTLE, AGNES, born 1773 in Dumfries-shire, wife of Andrew Cunningham, died at Gardner's Creek, New Brunswick, on 18 February 1824. [NBC.2.2.1824]

LITTLE, ANDREW, in Crawsknowe, testament 1790, Comm. Dumfries. [NRS]

LITTLE, ARCHIBALD, bon 22 December 1782, son of Reverend James Little and his wife Elizabeth Clark, died in Jamaica on 16 February 1804. [F.2.262]

LITTLE, ARCHIBALD, from Dumfries-shire, drowned at Wishart's Point, New Brunswick, on 2 June 1830. [GNS.29.6.1830]

LITTLE, JAMES, born 1822, son of James Little and his wife Helen Tennant in Wamphrey, Dumfries-shire, died in Jamaica in January 1851. [Wamphrey gravestone]

LITTLE, JAMES, born 1849, son of John Little and his wife Jane Beattie, died at Cross Lake, Manitoba, on 22 April 1879. [Westerkirk gravestone, Dumfries-shire]

LITTLE, JOHN, a merchant in Langholm, testament 1794, Comm. Dumfries. [NRS]

LITTLE, JOHN, in Souronne, testament 1798, Comm. Dumfries. [NRS]

LITTLE, MARGARET, widow of John Bell late of Scalehill, testament 1798, Comm. Dumfries. [NRS]

LIVINGSTONE, HUGH, born 1811, died in Port Hope, Upper Canada, on 12 January 1831. [Crossmichael gravestone, Dumfries-shire]

LOCKERBIE, AGNES, in Gilhall, Dumfries-shire, victim of assault in 1829. [NRS.AD14.29.211]

LOGAN, ADAM, born in Ayr, and his wife Margaret McNeil, emigrated to New York, parents of David Logan born there in 1804. [ANY]

LOGAN, FRANCIS, born 1752, died 5 June 1820, husband of Agnes Walker, born 1762, died 31 August 1835. [Dunlop gravestone, Ayrshire]

LOGAN, JOHN, born 1791 in Ayrshire, emigrated via Liverpool to Nova Scotia and from there to Philadelphia, Pennsylvania, naturalised in Washington on 5 June 1824. [D.C. District Court Records]

LOGAN, JOHN, messenger at arms in Greenock in 1849. [POD]

LOGAN, THOMAS, son of John Logan of Knockshinnoch and his wife Martha McAdam, died in the River St Lawrence, Canada, in 1813. [HAF]

LOGAN, WILLIAM, in Nether Aiket, born 1745, died 26 April 1816. [Dunlop gravestone, Ayrshire]

LOGAN, WILLIAM, in Clarkstone, Renfrewshire, dead by 1844, father of James Logan in Montreal, Quebec. [NRS.S/H]

LOGAN, …., master of the William and Ann of Annan trading between Beaumaris and Dumfries in 1824. [NRS.E504.9.10]

LOOKUP, ALEXANDER, born 1786 in Dumfries, Convenor of the Seven Incorporations there, a Magistrate of Dumfries, and an Elder of St Michael's Church there, died in Columbus, Texas, on 24 June 1849. [SG.1847]

LORIMER, JOHN, a stone dyker in Myers, Durrisdeer, Dumfries-shire, was accused of poaching in 1827. [NRS.JC26.1827.130]

LORIMER, THOMAS, in Glenwharrey, testament 1794, Comm. Dumfries. [NRS]

LORRAIN, WILLIAM, from Annandale, Dumfries-shire, a lime burner in Portland, St John, New Brunswick, probate 1804, N.B.

LOSH, JAMES, in Trinidad, only son of William Losh former factor to Ludovic Houston of Johnstone Castle, Renfrewshire, died in St Croix, Danish West Indies, on 22 February 1852. [W.1318]

LOTHIAN, RICHARD, of Staffold, residing in Dumfries, testament 1793, Comm. Dumfries. [NRS]

LOTTIMER, JAMES, a merchant in Ruthwell, testament 1792, Comm. Dumfries. [NRS]

LOW, ANDREW, master of the Farmer of Saltcoats from Greenock to Newfoundland in 1818; master of the Warner of Saltcoats from Greenock to Newfoundland in 1819. [NRS.E504.15.116/124]

LOWE, JOHN, born 1750 in Kenmure, Galloway, emigrated to America in 1771, settled in Fredericksburg, Virginia, as a teacher and later as an Episcopalian minister, died at Windsor Lodge, Va. In 1798. [TSA]

LOWDEN, JAMES, of Culmain, testament 1793, Comm. Dumfries. [NRS]

LOWDEN, Captain WILLIAM, born in Dumfries, settled in Nova Scotia around 1790, died in Pictou, N.S., on 20 February 1820. [AR.18.3.1820]

LOWDEN, ..., master of the Grace Gillespie of Dumfries trading with Ulverston in 1823. [NRS.E504.9.10]

LYLE, JOHN, formerly a merchant on Nevis, died in Greenock, Renfrewshire, testament 1791. [NRS.CC9.7.74]

LYON, DAVID, a mariner in Inverkip, testament, 1811, Comm. Glasgow. [NRS]

LYON, JEAN, born 1800, died 21 November 1883, wife of Thomas Hamilton, born 1797, died 1849, buried in Greenwood Cemetery, New York. [Newmilns gravestone, Ayrshire]

LYON, ROBERT, jr., born 1779, possibly from Renfrew, a gentleman at Northwest Arms, died 1 November 1819, probate 1819, Halifax, Nova Scotia.

LYON, WILLIAM, master of the Jessy of Ayr from Greenock to Savannah, Georgia, in 1818 and 1819. [NRS.E504.15.121/123]

MACADAM, JAMES, born 20 April 1809 in Maybole, Ayrshire, son of John MacAdam and his wife Janet Blane, a Lieutenant Colonel of the 33rd Bengal Native Infantry in India, died in England on 13 March 1888. [BA.3.104]

MCADAM, QUINTIN, son of Alexander McAdam of Grinnet, Ayrshire, died at Canandarque, USA, on 18 October 1853. [Inverness Advertiser: 15.11.1853]

MCALLISTER, ALEXANDER, born 1843, Lochryan lighthouse-keeper, died at Castlebank, Sanquhar, on 1 June 1919, husband of Mary Ann …., born 1848, died at Sanquhar, Dumfries-shire, on 9 August 1914. [Cairnryan gravestone, Wigtownshire]

MCALLISTER, PETER, in Whithorn, Wigtownshire, the victim of an assault in 1837. [NRS.AD14.37.218]

MACALPINE, JOHN, a surgeon in Glasgow, uncle of Jane MacAlpine, and of Margaret MacAlpine, his heirs, daughters of R. MacAlpine a surgeon in Norfolk, Virginia, 1827. [NRS.S/H]

MCALPINE, WILLIAM, born 1780 in Irvine, Ayrshire, cook aboard the Protector of St John, was drowned at St John, New Brunswick, on 13 May 1820. [CG.17.5.1820]

MCARA, JEAN, eldest daughter of James McAra a merchant in Largs, Ayrshire, married Thomas Walker, a surgeon from Kinross, in St Thomas, Danish West Indies, in 1813. [EA.5134.13]

MCARTHUR, ALEXANDER, a skipper in Greenock, testament, 1808, Comm. Glasgow. [NRS]

MCARTHUR, DUNCAN, was accused of theft but failed to turn up for trial, was outlawed in 1820. [NRS.JC26.1820.129]

MCARTHUR, Captain, master of the Albion of Greenock from the River Clyde bound for Montreal in 1850. [EEC.21946]

MCAULAY, ALEXANDER, a sailor in Ayr, testament, 1813, Comm. Glasgow. [NRS]

MCAULAY, DANIEL, oncast or putter below ground, of Quarry Green, St Quivox, Ayrshire, was, with others, accused of murder, mobbing, rioting, and assault with firearms at the Old Foundry, West Hawkhill farm, St Quivox, Ayrshire, in 1843. [NRS.AD14.43.375]

MACBETH, JAMES, born 1810 in Dalrymple, Ayrshire, son of James MacBeth a surgeon in Newtown-on-Ayr, emigrated to America in 1850. [F.3.422]

MCBRAIR, WILLIAM, born 1786, son of William McBrair, [1735-1821], and his wife Margaret Thomson, [1754-1841], died in Jamaica on 19 October 1818. [Colvend gravestone, Kirkcudbrightshire]

MCBRYDE, DUNCAN, a skipper in Greenock, testament, 1820, Comm. Glasgow. [NRS]

MCBRIDE, Captain, master of the Margaret of Greenock from Greenock with passengers bound for Quebec and Montreal in 1843. [GA.5912]

MCBURNIE, JOHN, in Druidville, testament 1794, Comm. Dumfries. [NRS]

MCBURNIE, ROBERT, in Druidville, testament 1797, Comm. Dumfries. [NRS]

MCCAIG, LIZZIE, born 1846 in Paisley, Renfrewshire, married William Allan in Bloomfield,] New Jersey, on 18 February 1869, died in Brooklyn, New York, on 19 September 1888. [EFR]

MCCALLUM, DANIEL CRAIG, born 1815 in Johnstone, Renfrewshire, emigrated with is parents to Rochester, New York, an engineer, died in 1878.

MCCALLUM, JAMES, Secretary of the Hibernian Protestant Emigration Society in Paisley, applied to settle in Canada on 17 February 1827. [TNA.CO384.5.1001]

MCCALLUM, Mrs MARGARET, born 1801, daughter of Robert Gardner in Irvine, Ayrshire, wife of Duncan McCallum, died in St Ann's, Jamaica, on 27 January 1830. [St Ann's gravestone]

MCCANN, JAMES, born 4 February 1799 in Greenock, a merchant in Jamaica, died there on 13 March 1832. [Scots cemetery gravestone, Jamaica]

MCCARLIE, JAMES, born 1814, died 2 August 1894, brother of John McCarlie, farmer in Pulryan, also of Jane McCarlie, born 1810, died 29 May 1892. [Cairnryan gravestone, Wigtownshire]

MCCARTNEY, ANDREW, a gardener in Dumfries, testament 1793, Comm. Dumfries. [NRS]

MCCARTNEY, JANET, widow of William Maxwell of Kirkland, testament 1800, Comm. Dumfries. [NRS]

MCCARTNEY, SAMUEL, born 1780 in Kirkcudbright, a merchant, applied to become a citizen of South Carolina on 24 June 1805. [NARA]

MCCARTNEY, WILLIAM, land surveyor in Knockshinnoch, Irongray, testament 1795, Comm. Dumfries. [NRS]

MCCASKIE, JAMES, in Santa Domingo, who died in Fort Jeremy, Santa Domingo, on 7 June 1798, son of James McCaskie a candlemaker in Dumfries, testament, 1799. [NRS.CC8.8.131]

MCCAUL, ALEXANDER, born 1790, son of Thomas McCaul, [1744-1795], and his wife Marion McNaught, [1766-1798], died on Chiswick Estate, St Thomas-in-the-East, Jamaica, in December 1816. [Dalry gravestone]

MCCAW, PETER, a mariner from Galloway, was admitted as a citizen of South Carolina, on 14 November 1797. [NARA.M1183.1]

MCCAW, THOMAS, a merchant in Montreal, Quebec, died in October 1865. [Colmonell gravestone, Ayrshire]

MCCAW, WILLIAM, MD, died in Mauritius on 16 March 1843. [Colmonell gravestone, Ayrshire]

MCCAW, WILLIAM, son of Robert McCaw [1817-1876] and his wife Jessie McTier, [1820-1901], died in Illinois aged 68. [Colmonell gravestone, Ayrshire]

MCCLELLAN, ROBERT, in Burnside of Kirkgunzion, testament 1796, Comm. Dumfries. [NRS]

MCCLELLAND, THOMAS, agent of the Bank of Scotland in Ayr, in 1849. [POD]

MCCLURE, WILLIAM, born 1800 in St Quivox, Ayrshire, son of William McClure a schoolmaster, was educated at Glasgow University, a minister in Nassau, the Bahamas, from 1837 until his death on 10 March 1863. [F.7.66]

MCCONNELL, HENRY, born 1794, a cotton spinner of Underwood Mill, Johnstone, Renfrewshire, later in New Sneddon Street, Paisley, was accused of discharging a firearm at Alexander Fisher in Johnstone, in 1820. [NRS.AD14.20.3]

MCCONCHIE, SAMUEL, born 1781 in Galloway, a merchant, was admitted as a citizen of South Carolina on 2 March 1807. [NARA.M1183.1]

MCCONACHIE, ELIZABETH, in Gatehouse of Fleet, widow of Robert Kerr in Jamaica, testament, 1814, Comm. Kirkcudbright. [NRS]

MCCONOCHIE, JAMES, son of William McConachie, [1754-1832], died in Tobago on 30 December 1826. [Balmaghie gravestone, Kirkcudbrightshire]

MCCORKINDALE, JOHN, in Johnstone, Renfrewshire, applied to settle in Canada on 4 March 1815. [NRS.RH9]

MCCORMACK, THOMAS, born 1786 in Dumfries, the manager of the Golden Grove Estate, St Thomas, Jamaica, died 13 December 1848. [St Andrew's gravestone, Jamaica]MCCORMICK, WILLIAM, born 1796 in Galloway, a grocer in Charleston, South Carolina, applied for naturalisation on 6 March 1822. [NARA.M1183.1]

MCCORQUENDALE, THOMAS, born 1796 in Dumfries-shire, emigrated to Canada in 1821, was granted land in Caverhill, New Brunswick. [PANB]

MCCOSH, JAMES, agent of the Western Bank of Scotland in Dalry, Ayrshire, in 1849. [POD]

MCCOSH, JAMES, born 1 April 1811 in Carskeoch, died in Princeton, New Jersey, on 16 November 1894. [Straiton gravestone, Ayrshire]

MCCRACKEN, PETER, born 1797, formerly a Sergeant of the 2nd Royal Regiment in Bombay, India, died in Maybole, Ayrshire, on 31 August 1863. [Colmonell gravestone, Ayrshire]

MCCRACKEN, ROBERT, born 1732, farmer in Strabacken, died on 20 April 1809, husband of Margaret Bell, born 1753, died on 24 June 1841. [Colmonell gravestone, Ayrshire]

MCCRACKEN, ROBERT, born 1770, died in Ardwell on 19 December 1831, husband of Martha Earl, born 1781, died 17 February 1840, parents of Grace McCracken who died in Melbourne, Victoria, Australia, on 19 April 1859, husband of A. McGeoch. [Colmonell gravestone, Ayrshire]

MCCRACKEN, ROBERT, born 1777 in Newton Douglas, Galloway, a merchant in Richmond, Virginia, was naturalised there on 19 September 1799. [VSA.15]

MCCRACKEN, WILLIAM, born 1772, in Auchincrosh, died 23 March 1844, husband of Grace Murray, born 1793, died 23 June 1875, parents of William McCracken, born 1827, died in New Zealand in October 1884. [Colmonell gravestone, Ayrshire]

MCCRAE, JOHN, son of James McCrae, [1765-1839], and his wife Janet Galbraith, [1776-1857], died in Paris, Canada West, on 21 February 1845. [Carsphairn gravestone, Kirkcudbrightshire]

MCCRAE, ROBERT, son of James McCrae, [1765-1839], and his wife Janet Galbraith, [1776-1857], died in Colborn, America, on 6 October 1869. [Carsphairn gravestone, Kirkcudbrightshire]

MCCREADIE, DAVID, in Rispin, Whithorn, Wigtownshire, the victim of an assault in 1837. [NRS.AD14.37.218]

MCCREADIE, HUGH, born 1815, a sailor, son of Hugh McCreadie a cartwright in Whithorn, Wigtownshire, was accused of several assaults in 1837. [NRS.AD14.37.218]

MCCREADY, Mrs JANET, wife of Hugh McCready from Maybole, Ayrshire, died in Montreal, Quebec, on 21 July 1832. [AJ.4422]

MCCREDIE, ANDREW, born 1757 in Ayrshire, son of William McCredie of Pierceton and his wife Barbara Wilson, a shipmaster and merchant in Savanna, Georgia, died there on 17 April 1807. [ANY][Savanna Death Register][CMSA.24.4.1807]

MCCREDIE, HUGH, born 1811, son of John McCredie, [1777-1831], a joiner who died in Mackay, Queensland, Australia, on 4 April 1882. [Ballantrae gravestone]

MCCREATH, JOHN, born 1777 in Urr, Kirkcudbrightshire, settled in Highgate, Westmoreland, Jamaica, died on 15 March 1865. [Grange Hill gravestone, Jamaica]

MCCRONE, HUGH, born 1787 in Ayrshire, died in Montreal, Quebec, on 5 February 1855. [QCG]

MCCULLOCH, HAWTHORN, born 1772 in Glasserton, Wigtownshire, son of Andrew McCulloch and his wife Grissel Shadlin, emigrated via Greenock to New York in 1802, settled in Clinton, Rennsseleur County, New York, husband of Christina McFarlan. [BAF]

MCCULLOCH, JOSEPH WEIR, born 1788, son of John McCulloch and his wife Elizabeth Murray in Lochmaben, Dumfries-shire, a surgeon who died in Kingston, Jamaica, on 7 August 1807. [Lochmaben gravestone]

MCCULLOCH, Reverend THOMAS, born 1776 in Neilston, Renfrewshire, was educated at Glasgow University, ordained in Stewarton, Ayrshire, on 13 June 1799, emigrated to Nova Scotia in 1803, a minister in Pictou, N.S., from 1802 to 1804, founder of Pictou Academy, Principal of Dalhousie College in Halifax, N.S., from 1838 until his death on 9 September 1843. [SF][HPC] [UPC]

MCCUNN, JAMES, a skipper in Greenock, testament, 1810, Comm. Glasgow. [NRS]

MCCURDIE, MARGARET, spouse of William Harvie, a manufacturer in Paisley, Renfrewshire, joint-heir of Thomas McCurdie, 1839. [NRS.GD1.500.63]

MCCURDIE, MARY, spouse of William Thomson a toll-keeper in Dundonald, Ayrshire, joint-heir of Thomas McCurdie, 1839. [NRS.GD1.500.63]

MCCUTCHEON, WILLIAM, born 1801 in Kells, Kirkcudbrightshire, a cattle jobber in Drumbreck, Balmaghie, was accused of cattle theft in 1832. [NRS.JC26.1832.29]

MCDAVID, JAMES, in Newton, Stewart, Dumfries-shire, father of James McDavid, born 1873, studied Divinity at Glasgow University, died in Buffalo, New York, on 4 January 1899. [S.17334]

MCDONALD, Captain ALEXANDER, born 1766, from Wigtown, Galloway, died in St John, New Brunswick, on 24 December 1812. [NBRG.28.12.1812]

MCDONALD, ALEXANDER, late in Jamaica, died in Greenock on 16 June 1840. [Nelson Street gravestone, Greenock]

MCDONALD, MIRIAM, daughter of John McDonald in Dumfries-shire, married Captain Edward H. Frank of the brig <u>Sarah of North Shields</u> in Liverpool, Kent County, New Brunswick, on 7 June 1827. [NBC.23.6.1827]

MCDONALD, NIEL, born 1822, a Free Church teacher in Barr, died 17 July 1858, father of Maggie McDonald, born 1843, wife of George Wilson, died in Wellington, New Zealand, on 1 June 1884. [Barr, Ayrshire, gravestone]

MCDONALD, RONALD, in Irvine, Ayrshire, Captain of the 44th Regiment, brother and heir of Alexander McDonald in Golden Spring, Jamaica, 1829. [NRS.S/H]

MCDOUGALL, GEORGE GORDON, born 1798, settled in St Croix, Danish West Indies, was drowned at Largs, Ayrshire, on 20 October 1835. [Largs gravestone]

MCDOWELL, ANDREW, from Galloway, a merchant in Charleston, South Carolina, was admitted as a citizen of S.C. on 3 January 1813. [NARA.M1183.1]

MCDOWALL, JAMES, son of William McDowall of Castle Semple, was educated at Glasgow University around 1764, died in St Lucia, British West Indies, on 30 May 1808. [Car.4.15]

MCDOUALL, JAMES, born 1752 in Wigtownshire, a merchant, was admitted as a citizen of South Carolina on 21 September 1807. [NARA.M1183.1]

MCDOWELL, PATE, born 1789 in Paisley, Renfrewshire, a weaver, who emigrated via Greenock to America, with his sons Matthew McDowell, born1814 in Glasgow, and William McDowell, born 1815 in Glasgow, was naturalised in New York on 23 April 1828. [NY Court of Common Pleas]

MCDOWELL, WILLIAM, of Gategill, an accountant in the Bank of Scotland in Dumfries, testaments, 1789, 1792, 1794, 1795 Comm. Dumfries. [NRS]

MCDOWELL, Captain, master of the Britannia of Dumfries from Dumfries bound for Miramachi, New Brunswick, in 1820, landed at Pictou, Nova Scotia. [DWJ.1.2.1820]

MCDUFF, WILLIAM, born 1837, son of Robert McDuff and his wife Agnes McCreath, died in New Zealand in 1880. [Ballantrae gravestone, Ayrshire]

MCEARCHIN, Captain, master of the Friendship of Greenock from Greenock bound for New Brunswick and Newfoundland in 1830. [GA.3140]

MCEUAN, ROBERT ANDREW, born 1815, son of Robert Andrew McEuan, [1781-1823], and his wife Jane Cochrane, [1789-1865], a merchant in Adelaide, South Australia, died in Greenock, Renfrewshire, on 13 November 1856. [Inverkip Street gravestone, Greenock]

MCCEWAN, MARY, wife of John McTaggart a merchant in Whithorn, Wigtownshire, sister and heir of William McEwan, a physician in Jamaica, 1791. [NRS.S/H]

MCEWAN, WILLIAM, master of the Venus of Port Patrick trading with Donaghadee in 1819. [NRS.E504.29.17]

MACEWING, Captain, master of the Gleniffer of Greenock trading between Greenock and Quebec in 1839. [SG.8.746]

MCFARLANE, ALEXANDER, in Kilburnie, Ayrshire, applied to settle in Canada on 27 February 1815. [NRS.RH9]

MCFARLANE, JAMES, a weaver in Girvan, Ayrshire, was accused of mobbing and rioting in 1817. [NRS.JC26.1817.225]

MACFARLANE, JOHN, born 1762 in Paisley, married Helen Barr, born 1773 in Scotland, emigrated to Boston, Massachusetts, in 1795, settled in Germantown, Pennsylvania, died 24 December 1820. [CMF]

MACFIE, DUGALD, born 1770 in Greenock, a merchant in Charleston, South Carolina, was admitted as a citizen of S.C. on 25 June 1812. [NARA.M1183.1]

MCGAW, ALEXANDER, born in May 1831 near Stranraer, Wigtownshire, emigrated to Canada in 1851, settled in Philadelphia, Pennsylvania, as a bridgebuilder in 1873, died there on 29 January 1905. [AP]

MCGAW, RICHARD, [1780-1867], and his wife Agnes McMurtrie, [1795-1873], parents of Richard B. McGaw in Hamburg, Germany. [Barr gravestone, Renfrewshire]

MCGEOCH, GRACE, from Glen Luce, Wigtownshire, emigrated via Belfast aboard the Lorenzo bound for New York on 2 May 1816. [NWI.2.361]

MCGEOCH, SAMUEL, from Glen Luce, Wigtownshire, emigrated via Belfast aboard the Lorenzo bound for New York on 2 May 1816. [NWI.2.361]

MCGEORGE, C., a messenger at arms in Dumfries in 1849. [POD]

MCGEORGE, JOHN, in Meikle Furthrad, Urr, Dumfries-shire, testament 1793, Comm. Dumfries. [NRS]

MCGEORGE, THOMAS, in Hermitage, Urr, Dumfries-shire, testament 1793, Comm. Dumfries. [NRS]

MCGHIE, EDWARD, born 1813, unemployed in Maxwelltown, Troquier, Stewartry of Kirkcudbright, was accused of housebreaking, theft, and reset at Hall of Drumpark, Irongray, Kirkcudbrightshire, in 1832. [NRS.AD14.32.57]

MCGHIE, FRANCIS ALEXANDER, born 20 November 1806 in Toull, died in Tuscaloosa, Alabama, on 20 August 1856. [Buittle gravestone, Kirkcudbrightshire]

MCGHIE, PHILIP, a skipper in Greenock, testament, 1823, Comm. Glasgow. [NRS]

MCGIBBON, Colonel JOHN, born 1794 in Paisley, emigrated to Canada in 1818, died in Dundee, Lower Canada, on 13 May 1848. [SG.1731]

MCGILL, ANTHONY, son of William McGill a shoemaker in Paisley, was educated at Glasgow University from 1812 to 1823, a minister who died in Barton, Ontario, on 3 February 1895. [MAGU]

MCGILL, JOHN, and his wife Mary, in Hillhead, Stranraer, Wigtownshire, were victims of theft in 1830. [NRS.AD14.3.122]

MCGILL, PETER, born in Dumfries or Galloway, emigrated to Canada in 1809, a merchant, banker, and politician, died at Beaver Hall Place, Montreal, Quebec, on 28 September 1860. [BCB]

MCGILL, Reverend ROBERT, born in Ayrshire, emigrated to Canada in 1829, a minister at Niagara from 1829 to 1845, minister at St Paul's, Montreal, Quebec, from 1845 to his death on 4 February 1856. [HPC]

MCGOWAN, ALEXANDER, master of the sloop Mary of Kirkcudbright, inventory, 1823, Comm. Kirkcudbright. [NRS]

MCGOWAN, GEORGE, of Garlieston, Wigtownshire, born 7 June 1774, emigrated with his family to Jamaica, died there in June 1824. [Car.5.39]

MCGOWAN, JAMES, born 1796, son of William McGowan, [1756-1831], and his wife Grizel Callendar, [1762-1813], a merchant in Castries, St Lucia, died on 25 February 1834. [Crossmichael gravestone, Dumfriesshire]

MCGOWAN, WILLIAM, born 1803, son of William McGowan, [1756-1831], and his wife Grizel Callendar, [1762-1813], a merchant in Castries, St Lucia, died on 1 January 1831. [Crossmichael gravestone, Dumfriesshire]

MCGREGOR, PETER, born 1788 in Greenock, Renfrewshire, was naturalised in New York on 7 April 1811. [NARA]

MCGUFFIE, ANTHONY, born 1783 in Galloway, a clerk in Charleston, was admitted as a citizen of South Carolina on 19 October 1813. [NARA.M1183.1]

MCHAFFIE, JOHN, a mariner in Stranraer, inventory, 1819, Comm. Wigtown. [NRS]

MCHOULL, ROBERT, son of William McHoull, [1783-1848], a merchant in Galston, Ayrshire, settled in Cartwright township, Canada. [Galston gravestone]

MCHUTCHESON, WILLIAM, born 1827 in Renfrew, son of James McHutcheson a merchant, was educated at Glasgow University, a minister at Banton, emigrated to New Zealand in 1857, died in Arrowtown, N.Z., on 2 February 1904. [F.3.371]

MCILDOE, ALEXANDER, born 1777, died in August 1854. [Dunlop gravestone, Ayrshire]

MCILWRAITH, JAMES, born 24 December 1789 in Johnstone, Renfrewshire, a weaver, married Euphemia Jean Stewart in 1815, and with three children settled in Ontario in 1821. [SG.27.4.148]

MCILWRAITH, JOHN, born 1808, drowned in New York on 12 August 1845. [Barr gravestone, Ayrshire]

MCILWRAITH, MARGARET, daughter of John McIlwraith and his wife Susanna Boag, wife of Duncan McGown, died in Alma township, Peel, Canada West, on 30 June 1871. [Greenock gravestone, Renfrewshire]

MCILWRAITH, ROBERT, born 1756 in Greenock, a merchant who died in Tobago in January 1798. [Inverkip gravestone, Greenock]

MCILWRICK, DAVID, born 1766, died in Altercannoch on 30 June 1832, husband of Helen McMurray, born 1779, died 10 June 1852, parents of David McIlwrick, born 1814, died 21 April 1844 in Knoxville, USA. [Colmonell gravestone]

MCINNES, JOHN T., born 24 March 1828 in Paisley, Renfrewshire, son of John McInnes and his wife Martha Hunter, settled in Philadelphia, Pennsylvania, in 1840, a quarry owner, died in Philadelphia on 5 March 1886. [AP]

MCINNES, JOHN, born 16 July 1833 in Linwood, Kilbarchan, Renfrewshire, was educated at the Ratisbon Seminary, Germany, in 1855, ordained as a Roman Catholic priest in 1862, to Canada in 1875. [SIG.296] [RSC.I.259]

MCINROY, WILLIAM, born 1819, son of Peter McInroy and hi wife Margaret McPherson, died in Trinidad on 9 November 1841. [Gourock gravestone]

MCINTYRE, JAMES, guilty of assault, was sentenced in Ayr to transportation to the colonies for seven years in 1813. [NRS.GD1.959]

MCILWRAITH, JOHN, born 1808, drowned off New York 12 August 1845. [Barr gravestone, Ayrshire]

MCIVER, DAVID, a skipper in Greenock, testament, 181, Comm. Glasgow. [NRS]

MCIVER, JOHN, eldest son of Charles McIver the harbourmaster of Greenock, died in Kingston, Jamaica, in 1804. [AJ.2970]

MCIVER, JOHN, from Greenock, settled in Columbia, South Carolina, around 1820, died in Alabama on 25 May 1833. [Telescope,18.6.1833]

MACK, D. J., agent of the Bank of Scotland in Ardrossan, Ayrshire, in 1849. [POD]

MCKANE, WILLIAM, born 1802 in Stranraer, Wigtownshire, a blacksmith in St Michael Street, Dumfries, was accused of theft at Kirkton, Dumfries-shire, in 1830. [NRS.AD14.30.131]

MCKAY, ALEXANDER, an Anti-Burgher and a grocer, was admitted as a burgess and guild-brother of Ayr on 23 October 1816. [ABR]

MACKAY, ALICE, wife of John Aitchison a merchant in the Virgin Islands, died in Tortula on 30 November 1797. [Cummertrees gravestone, Dumfries-shire]

MCKAY, JOHN, born 1815 in Maxwelltown, Dumfries-shire, died in New York on 31 December 1878. [AO]

MCKAY, ROBERT, born 1790, son of James McKay and his wife Ann Ferguson, [1771-1803], died in Concord, Tobago, in 1821. [Dumfries gravestone]

MCKAY, SAMUEL, born 1802, a weaver in Paisley, imprisoned in Glasgow accused of theft in 1820. [NRS.AD14.20.19]

MCKAY, WILLIAM, born 1813, son of John McKay, [1778-1851], died in Castries, St Lucia, on 5 June 1845. [Crossmichael gravestone. Dumfries-shire]

MCKUNE, WILLIAM, a butcher in Maxwelltown, Dumfries, was accused of sheep stealing in 1846. [NRS.AD14.46.301]

MCLEOD, EVAN, messenger at arms in Greenock in 1849. [PO]

MCKELLAR, ALEXANDER, a skipper in Greenock, testament, 18 Comm. Glasgow. [NRS]

MCKELLAR, JOHN, a mariner in Greenock, testament, 1801, Comm. Glasgow. [NRS]

MCKELLAR, PETER, a skipper in Greenock, testament, 1815, Comm. Glasgow. [NRS]

MCKELVIE, ARCHIBALD, a skipper in Ayr, testament, 1812, Comm. Glasgow. [NRS]

MCKELVIE, JOHN, master of the <u>Woods of Irvine</u> from Greenock to Newfoundland in 1818. [NRS.E504.15.122]

MCKENN, JAMES, at Troqueer Gate, testament 1800, Comm. Dumfries. [NRS]

MCKENNA, GILBERT, in Lagganholm, Ayrshire, a decreet, 1815. [NRS.CS34.12.107]

MACKENZIE, ANDREW LAING, born 1839, son of John MacKenzie, a miller, and his wife Janet Laing, died on 15 January 1847, buried in Antigua. [Greenock gravestone]

MCKENZIE, JAMES, in Irvine, Ayrshire, a sequestration petition, 1845. [NRS.CS279.1298]

MCKENZIE, JOHN, a skipper in Greenock, testament, 1822, Comm. Glasgow. [NRS]

MCKENZIE, JOHN, born 1797, 'for 25 years was the Beadle of Loch Ryan Church, died 8 December 1879. [Cairnryan gravestone, Wigtownshire]

MACKERGO, WILLIAM, born 23 October 1829 in Kilmarnock, Ayrshire, graduated MA from Glasgow University in 1849, a minister in New York from 1872 to 1895, graduated DD from Yale in 1872, LL.D. from Princeton in 1883, and DD from Amherst in 1872, died in February 1895. [MAGU]

MCKERROW, M., agent of the Bank of Scotland in Cumnock, Ayrshire, in 1849. [POD]

MACKIE, ALEXANDER, born 1818, died in Sheldon, Houston, Minnesota, on 27 December 1866. [Barr gravestone, Ayrshire]

MACKIE, Captain JOHN, from Dalry, Ayrshire, master of the brig <u>Ann of St John</u>, New Brunswick, probate 1806, N.B.

MCKIE, JOHN, born 1798, son of Peter McKie, a farmer in Morrach, Whithorn, and his wife Margaret Rodie, died in Antigua on 14 November 1821. [Whithorn gravestone, Wigtownshire]

MCKIE, PETER, son of James McKie, [1725-1789], in Dumfries, settled in Philadelphia, Pennsylvania. [Dumfries gravestone]

MCKIE, WILLIAM, son of James McKie, [1725-1789], settled in Philadelphia, Pennsylvania. [Dumfries gravestone]

MCKINLEY, ALEXANDER, a wright in Dalmellington, Ayrshire, died 5 October 1829, father of William McKinley in Elizabeth, New Jersey, [NRS.S/H]

MCKINLAY, ROBERT, a skipper in Greenock, testament, 1801, Comm. Glasgow. [NRS]

MCKINLAY, Captain, master of the Cruikston Castle of Greenock from Greenock with passengers bound for Quebec in 1840 also to Cape Breton in 1840. [GA]

MCKINNEE, GILBERT, born 1752 in Galloway, a Loyalist in 1783, son of William McKinnee who was lost from the Countess of Dalhousie, died at Carlton Village, near Shelburne, Nova Scotia, on 6 February 1821. [AR.24.2.1821]

MCKINNELL, ROBERT, master of the Swallow of Dumfries trading with Liverpool in 1828. [NRS.E504.9.10]

MCKIRDY, BERNARD, born 1790, a labourer in Inverkip, Renfrewshire, with his wife and family, applied to settle in Canada in April 1827. [TNA.CO384.5.979]

MCKISSOCK, JAMES, a mariner in Stranraer, testament, 1822, Comm. Wigtown. [NRS]

MCKISSOCK, JOHN, formerly an innkeeper in Girvan, Ayrshire, was admitted as a burgess and freeman of Ayr on 20 December 1826. [ABR]

MCKNAIGHT, THOMAS, in Grenada, a sasine in 1791. [NRS.RS.Wigtown.287]

MCKNAUGHT, THOMAS, born 1834, son of Thomas McKnaught, [1819-1867], died in New York on 14 November 1869. [Wigtown gravestone]

MCKNIGHT, SAMUEL, born 1801 in Galloway, an accountant in Charleston, South Carolina, applied to be naturalised on 20 April 1825. [NARA.M1183.1]

MCLACHLAN, ALEXANDER, son of William McLachlan and his wife Anne McGhie in Kirkcudbright, in Dominica in 1787. [EUL. Laing Charters.3268]

MCLACHLAN, CORNELIUS, born 1773, son of William McLachlan, [1736-1801], and his wife Sarah Smith, [1733-1818], died in Port Royal, Jamaica, on 14 July 1795. [Colvend gravestone, Kirkcudbrightshire]

MCLACHLAN, JOHN, a skipper in Greenock, testament, 1804, Comm. Glasgow. [NRS]

MCLACHLAN, PHILIP, born 1817, a drawboy, in New Sneddon Street, Paisley, was accused of theft in 1831. [NRS.AD14.31.182]

MCLAGGAN, JOHN, born 1807, son of James McLaggan and his wife Elizabeth Ireland, [1778-1816], died in St John's, New Brunswick, on 20 January 1820. [Balmaghie gravestone, Kirkcudbrightshire]

MACLAREN, JAMES, son of Reverend John MacLaren and his wife Magdalene Cochrane, died at Montego Bay, Jamaica, in September 1823. [Kilbarchan gravestone, Renfrewshire]

MCLEA, KENNETH, from Greenock, Renfrewshire, agent for Messrs James Stewart and Company of Greenock and of St John's, Newfoundland, married Elizabeth Brine, daughter of John Brine in St John's, NFD., there on 9 September 1829. [RGNA.15.9.1829]

MCLEA, DANIEL, master of the <u>Victory of Ayr</u> trading with Dublin, Ireland, in 1818. [NRS.E504.4.14]

MCLEAN, ALLAN, born 1824, youngest son of John McLean a merchant in Greenock, died in Trinidad in 1838. [SG.741]

MCLEAN, JAMES, a skipper in Irvine, Ayrshire, testament, 1802, Comm. Glasgow. [NRS]

MCLEAN, JOHN, born 1774, son of ....McLean and his wife Janet Richardson in Anwoth, Kirkcudbrightshire, died in Nassau, New Providence, the Bahamas, in 1799. [Anwoth gravestone]

MCLELLAN, JOHN, a messenger at arms in Annan, Dumfries-shire, in 1849. [POD]

MCLELLAN, THOMAS, agent of the City of Glasgow Bank in Barrhead, Renfrewshire, in 1849. [POD]

MCLELLAN, WILLIAM H., agent in Kirkcudbright, for the Bank of Scotland in 1849. [POD]

MCLEOD, EVAN, messenger at arms in Greenock in 1849. [POD]

MCLEOD, JOHN, a skipper in Paisley, testament, 1821, Comm. Glasgow. [NRS]

MCLURE, WILLIAM, born 1763 in Ayr, settled in Philadelphia, Pennsylvania, in 1796, a merchant and geologist, died 1840. [SSA]

MCMASTER, DANIEL, born 1753 in Galloway, a mariner in St Andrews, New Brunswick, probate, 1806, N.B.

MCMEEKAN, JEAN, widow of Robert McCandlish a mason at the Bridgend of Dumfries, testament 1792, Comm. Dumfries. [NRS]

MCMEIKINE, ROBERT, son of Gilbert McMeikine a merchant in Glen Luce, Wigtownshire, and his wife Jean McHaffie, a merchant in Kingston, Jamaica, a sasine in 1801. [NRS.RS.Wigtown.623]

MCMICHAEL, JAMES, born 1772 in Muirkirk, Ayrshire, son of George McMichael, emigrated to Pennsylvania in 1793, settled in Townsend, Norfolk County, Ontario, in 1820, died 9 September 1821. [BAF]

MCMICKEN, JOHN, master of the <u>Commerce of Ayr</u> from Greenock to Quebec in 1814. [NRS.E504.15.104]

MCMIKING, ROBERT, a skipper in Laigh Salchrie, inventory, 1822, Comm. Wigtown. [NRS]

MCMILLAN, JAMES, son of John McMillan, [1777-1835], and his wife Ann Barker, [1760-1842], in Whithorn, Galloway, died on St Vincent aged 28. [Whithorn gravestone]

MCMILLAN, JAMES, President of the Hibernian Protestant Emigration Society in Paisley, applied to settle in Canada on 17 February 1827. [TNA.CO384.5.101]

MCMILLAN, JOHN, born 1769, son of Robert McMillan, [1749-1790], and his wife Margaret Donaldson, died in Fayetteville, North Carolina, on 7 October 1820. [Dumfries gravestone]

MCMILLAN, JOHN, born 1783 in Newton Stewart, Galloway, a merchant, was naturalised in South Carolina on 11 May 1810. [NARA.M1183.1]

MCMINN, CHARLES, in Dumfries, a victim of arson in 1845, [NRS.AD14.45.149]; a messenger at arms in Dumfries in 1849. [POD]

MCMORROW, or MURRAY, MICHAEL, born 1816, a collier of Gordon Street, Ayr, was, with others, accused of murder, mobbing, rioting, and assault with firearms at the Old Foundry, West Hawkhill farm, St Quivox, Ayrshire, in 1843. [NRS.AD14.43.375]

MCMURDO, CHARLES, aboard HMS Amarillo, son of Captain George McMurdo of the Dumfries Militia, died in Dominica in December 1808. [SM.71.158]

MCMURDO, ROBERT, a merchant and brewer in Dumfries, testament, 1790, Comm. Dumfries. [NRS]

MCMURLAND, ANDREW, master of the Elizabeth of Ayr trading with Belfast in 1818 [NRS.E504.4.14]

MCMURRAY, JAMES, a skipper in Stranraer, inventory, 1801, Comm. Wigtown. [NRS]

MCNAUGHT, JOHN, in Urioch, Balmaghie, Kirkcudbrightshire, a victim of cattle theft in 1832. [NRS.JC26.1832.29]

MCNAUGHTON, DANIEL, son of Donald McNaughton a merchant in Greenock, settled in Montreal, Quebec, before 1817. [NRS.SC53.56.1]

MCNAUGHTON, WILLIAM, born 8 November 1820, a fur trader in New York, died in Brooklyn, N.Y., on 6 February 1879. [ANY]

MCNEEL, SAMUEL, born 1784 in Whithorn, Galloway, a merchant in Charleston, South Carolina, was admitted as a citizen of S.C. on 25 June 1812. [NARA.M1183.1]

MCNEILL, Major ALEXANDER, in North Carolina, a letter to his kinsman Lieutenant General Duncan Darroch of Gourock, Renfrewshire, 1835. [NLS.Acc.9722]

MCNEILL, JOHN, born 1818, died 13 July 1908, husband of Grace McCutcheon, who died on 9 July 1905. [Cairnryan gravestone, Wigtownshire]

MCNEIL, NATHAN, in Whithorn, Wigtownshire, a letter dated 1831. [NRS.GD174.1689]

MCPHERSON, ALEXANDER, a mariner in Greenock, testament, 1803, Comm. Glasgow. [NRS]

MCPHERSON, ARCHIBALD, a skipper in Greenock, testament, 1803, Comm. Glasgow. [NRS]

MCPHERSON, PETER, born 1789 in Greenock, Renfrewshire, a tallow chandler in Charleston, South Carolina, was naturalised in S.C. on 5 July 1811. [NARA.M1183.

MCQUAKER, WILLIAM, born 1730, died in July 1800, husband of Janet McConnal, born 1743, died in June 1772. [Colmonell gravestone]

MCQUEEN, J. W., agent in Sanquhar, Dumfries-shire, for the British Linen Company in 1849. [POD]

MCQUHAE, RICHARD, born 21 December 1766, son of Reverend William McQhuae and his wife Elizabeth Park in St Quivox, Ayrshire, died in Jamaica on 9 March 1805. [F.3.66]

MCTAGGART, ISAAC, born 1804, son of James McTaggart, [1757-1832], and his wife Mary Sproat, [1761-1829], died in Ottawa, Ontario, on 18 December 1861. [Senwick gravestone, Kirkcudbrightshire]

MACTAGGART, JOHN, formerly a Civil Engineer on the Rideau Canal in Canada, an author, died in Tors, Kirkcudbright, on 8 January 1830. [GM.100.285]

MCTIER, DAVID, born 1802 in Wigtownshire, died in Halifax, Nova Scotia, on 15 June 1840. [HJ.22.6.1840]

MCTURK, WALTER, a surgeon in Sanquhar, Dumfries-shire, testament 1794, Comm. Dumfries. [NRS]

MCVICAR, ALEXANDER, born 1770, son of John McVicar and his wife Mary Murray in Lochmaben, Dumfries-shire, died in Port Royal, Jamaica, on 23 January 1796. [Lochmaben gravestone]

MCWHINNIE, ISABELLA, second daughter of William McWhinnie a merchant, married John Paul from Charleston, South Carolina, in Kirkcudbright on 27 July 1829. [BM.26.841]

MCWHINNIE, ROBERT, in Strand Street, Kilmarnock, Ayrshire, a former soldier of the 36th Regiment, applied to settle in Canada on 14 April 1827. [TNA.CO384.5.971]

MCWHINNIE, WILLIAM, eldest son of David McWhinnie in Ayr, a planter who died on Whitehall Estate, St Mary's, Jamaica, in 1806. [AJ.3094]

MCWHINNIE, WILLIAM, born 1801 in Galloway, a merchant in Charleston, South Carolina, was naturalised in S.C. in 17 March 1828. [NARA.M1183.1]

MCWHIRTER, THOMAS, born 1821, son of John McWhirter [1769-1840] husband of Elizabeth McConnachie, [1784-1839], died in Heathcot, Victoria, Australia, on 27 January 1868. [Colmonell gravestone, Ayrshire]

MCWILLIAMS, ARCHIBALD, from Ayr, applied to become a citizen of South Carolina on 3 July 1787. [NARA]

MCWILLIAM, JOHN, master of the sloop <u>Dumfries of Dumfries</u>, testament, 1826, Comm. Dumfries. [NRS]

MCWILLIAM, J., messenger at arms in Stranraer, Wigtownshire, in 1849. [POD]

MABEN, MATTHEW, from Dumfries, emigrated to America before 1822, a merchant in Virginia. [OD]

MAIR, HUGH, born 16 July 1797, son of Archibald Mair a gentleman in Newmilns, Ayrshire, was educated at Glasgow University from 1811 until 1818, later a minister at Fort Miller, Northumberland County, New York, in 1825, in Johnstown, N.Y., from 1830 until 1843, and in Waterloo, Canada, from 1847 until his death there on 1 November 1854. [MAGU]

MAITLAND, DAVID, born 1846 in Kirkcudbright, declared his intention to naturalise in Virginia on 14 May 1872. [Norfolk Borough Court Records, Va.]

MAITLAND, JOHN, a butcher, son of John Maitland a butcher burgess and freeman of Ayr, was admitted as a burgess and freeman of Ayr on 24 September 1800. [ABR]

MAITLAND, MARGARET, residing at the College of Lincluden, testament 1798, Comm. Dumfries. [NRS]

MAITLAND, STUART CAIRNS, of Dundrennan, Dumfries-shire, died in Dresden, Germany, on 4 December 1861. [W.XXII.2364]

MALCOLM, ARCHIBALD, conjunct town clerk of Dumfries, testament 1795, Comm. Dumfries. [NRS]

MALCOLM, JAMES, son of James Malcolm a weaver in Largs, Ayrshire, was educated at Marischal College, Aberdeen, in 1853, later a schoolmaster in Melbourne, Victoria, Australia. [MCA]

MALCOLM, JOHN, in Irvine, Ayrshire, disposed of land in East Back Road, Irvine, to James Cowan a candlemaker there in 1845. [NRS]

MANDERSTON, NICOLAS HUNTER, youngest daughter of Mark Manderston in Dumfries, married W. Williams in St George, Grenada, on 2 May 1837. [S.1821]

MANN, HUGH, messenger at arms, Ayr, 1849. [POD]

MARTIN, ALEXANDER, born 1808, died in Pittston, North America, on 16 March 1871. [Carsphairn gravestone, Dumfries-shire]

MARTIN, DONALD, in Greenock, a former soldier of the 21st Regiment of Foot, with his wife and two children, applied to settle in Canada on 15 March 1819. [TNA.CO384.5.101]

MARTIN, ELIZABETH, spouse of Reverend David Donaldson minister at Wamphrey, testament 1791, Comm. Dumfries. [NRS]

MARTIN, ISABELLA, born 1807, daughter of James Martin, [1734-1806], married Alexander Brown, and died in Madison, Indiana, on 3 September 1858. [Borgue gravestone, Kirkcudbrightshire]

MARTIN, JANET, third daughter of James Martin of Highlaw, Dumfries-shire, widow of James Hervey in Chicago, Illinois, died in Montreal, Quebec, in 1857. [EEC.23023]

MARTIN, JOHN, in Little Airdrie, testament 1796, Comm. Dumfries. [NRS]

MARTIN, JOHN, master of the <u>Diana of Dumfries</u> from Carsethorn, Dumfries-shire, bound for Prince Edward Island and New Brunswick in 1821. [DCr.30.1.1821]

MARTIN, ROBERT, in Straith, Glencairn, testament 1800, Comm. Dumfries. [NRS]

MARTIN, ROBERT, a pedlar from Ayrshire, died in Cumberland County, Nova Scotia, on 5 February 1819. [HJ.15.2.1819]

MARTIN, SAMUEL, born 1813, died in Laurenburg, Indiana, on 25 May 1867. [Borgue gravestone, Kirkcudbrightshire]

MATHER, JAMES, miller at Clouden, testament 1797, Comm. Dumfries. [NRS]

MATTHEWS, PETER, a labourer in Girvan, Ayrshire, was accused of mobbing and rioting in 1817. [NRS.JC26.1817.225]

MAULE, Lieutenant THOMAS, in Dumfries, testament 1791, Comm. Dumfries. [NRS]

MAXWELL, ALEXANDER, youngest son of Lieutenant Colonel Maxwell of Carruchen, died in Galt, Upper Canada, on 1 August 1834. [AJ.4525]

MAXWELL, ANDREW, born 1793 in Renfrewshire, took the Oath of Allegiance on26 August 1833. [Norfolk Borough Court Records, Virginia]

MAXWELL, Major BRYCE, son of Provost Edward Maxwell and his wife Charlotte Blair, died on Martinique in 1809. [St Michael's gravestone, Dumfries]

MAXWELL, EDWARD, late Provost of Dumfries, testament 1791, Comm. Dumfries. [NRS]

MAXWELL, JAMES, in Gatehouse of Fleet, Kirkcudbrightshire, a former soldier of the Royal Artillery, with his wife and five children, applied to settle in Canada on 16 March 1827. [TNA.CO384.5.593]

MAXWELL, JOHN, at the Bridgend of Dumfries, testament 1796, Comm. Dumfries. [NRS]

MAXWELL, JOHN, born in July 1774, son of Reverend Thomas Maxwell and his wife Elizabeth Brown in Stewarton, Ayrshire, a surgeon in the West Indies, died on 13 July 1805. [F.3.126]

MAXWELL, JOHN HAY, born 1839, from Ayr, died in Ottawa, Canada, on 8 July 1873. [GH.10529]

MAXWELL, ROBERT, of Boatford, testament 1795, Comm. Dumfries. [NRS]

MAXWELL, ROBERT, of Castlehill, late Provost of Lochmaben, testament 1793/1795, Comm. Dumfries. [NRS]

MAXWELL, ROBERT, of Glenarn, testament 1794, Comm. Dumfries. [NRS]

MAXWELL, ROBERT, late Provost of Dumfries, testament 1797, Comm. Dumfries. [NRS]

MAXWELL, ROBERT, master of the <u>Fame of Ayr</u> trading with Dublin in 1818. [NRS.E504.4.14]

MAXWELL, ROBERT, born 9 February 1777 in Stewarton, Ayrshire, son of Reverend Thomas Maxwell and his wife Elizabeth Brown, died in Tobago on 26 November 1802. [F.3.126]

MAXWELL, THOMAS, born 19 December 1775 in Stewarton, Ayrshire, son of Reverend Thomas Maxwell and his wife Elizabeth Brown, died in Tobago on 26 November 1802. [F.3.126]

MAXWELL, WILLIAM, in East Blackshaw, testament 1790, Comm. Dumfries. [NRS]

MAXWELL, WILLIAM, in Clonyeard, testament 1794, Comm. Dumfries. [NRS]

MAYWOOD, ROBERT CAMPBELL, born 1786 in Greenock, an actor in New York in 1819, theatre manager in Philadelphia, Pennsylvania, from 1832 until 1840, died in Troy, N.Y., in 1856. [TSA]

MEIKLE, WILLIAM, farmer in Oldhall, born 1802, died 8 July 1853, husband of Mary Picken, born 1803, died 14 February 1886. [Dunlop gravestone, Ayrshire]

MELVILLE, WILLIAM, son of Alexander Melville of Hallfields, Fife, [1784-1842], and his wife Grace Babington, [1779-1823], died in Austin, Texas, aged 25. [Dumfries gravestone]

MENTEITH, CHARLES GRANVILLE STUART, in Closeburn, Dumfries-shire, a victim of poachers in 1832. [NRS.AD14.32.81]

METHVEN, JAMES, son of Reverend James Methven in Stewarton, Ayrshire, was educated at Glasgow University in 1819, emigrated to America. [MAGU]

MILLER, ALEXANDER, a merchant in Greenock, partner in the firm of Miller, Ferguson and Company, merchants in Newfoundland in 1823. [NRS.CS44.1824]

MILLER, ANDREW, born 1802, a weaver in Paisley, imprisoned in Glasgow accused of theft in 1820. [NRS.AD14.20.19]

MILLER, D., master of the <u>Jessie Stevens of Irvine</u> from Glasgow with passengers bound for Quebec in 1848. [GCA.TCN.26/3]

MILLER, FRANCIS, a mariner from Ayrshire, was admitted as a citizen of S.C. on 13 April 1797. [NARA.M1183.1]

MILLER, GEORGE, born 1775 in Dumfries, a clock and watchmaker in St John, New Brunswick, died in Boston, Massachusetts, on 9 September 1830. [NBC.11.9.1830]

MILLER, GEORGE, born 1802, for 25 years a master at Montego Bay Academy, St James, Jamaica, died in Kilbarchan, Renfrewshire, on 21 November 1873. [Kilbarchan East gravestone]

MILLER, GEORGE CUMMING, a Captain of the 54th Regiment of Foot, brother of Sir William Miller of Glenlee, Kirkcudbrightshire, married Lucy Masterman, daughter of John Masterman, in Antigua on 18 June 1850. [AJ.5349]

MILLER, JAMES, son of John Miller in Loudoun, Ayrshire, was educated at Glasgow University in 1820, later was a preacher in USA, died in St Charles, Iowa, on 26 January 1867. [MAGU]

MILLER, JAMES, from Newmilns, Ayrshire, a divinity student in 1823, emigrated to America. [AUPC]

MILLER, JOHN, an Anti-Burgher and a baker, was admitted as a burgess and guilds-brother of Ayr on 18 September 1816. [ABR]

MILLAR, JOHN, from Dalton, Dumfriesshire, with 7 children, emigrated to Canada in 1834 settled in Edwardsburgh, Grenville County, Ontario. [LAC.MG24.I67]

MILLAR, JOHN, a merchant in Kingston, Jamaica, later in Muirsheal, Renfrewshire, died in 1854. [NRS.NRAS.0623.JMT, bundle 2]

MILLER, MATTHEW, in 13 Cotton Street, Paisley, applied to settle in Canada on 12 May 1827. [TNA.CO384.5.991]

MILLER, ROBERT, agent in Stewarton, Ayrshire, for the Union Bank of Scotland in 1849. [POD]

MILLER, Captain WILLIAM T., from Saltcoats, Ayrshire, a mariner in Bathurst, New Brunswick, master of the brig Margaret Ritchie, died in Bathurst on 16 September 1832, probate, 1832, N.B. [NBC.13.10.1832]

MILLAR, WILLIAM, born 1774, a millwright, died 1 May 1850, husband of Marion Aird, born 1800, died 2 March 1885. [Riccarton gravestone, Ayrshire]

MILLER, WILLIAM, born 2 July 1798 in Troon, Ayrshire, married Mary Watson in Irvine, Ayrshire, on 2 July 1819, parents of John Miller born 1820, settled in Bonaventure County, Quebec in 1825. [SG.32.2.61/200]

MILLAR, WILLIAM, born 1801, son of Hugh Millar, [1749-1824], and his wife Jean ...., [1761-1830], died in Grenada on 23 March 1833. [Kilmaurs gravestone, Ayrshire]

MILLER, Reverend WILLIAM, born 1786 in Ayrshire, emigrated to Nova Scotia in 1821, was ordained at West River, Pictou, N.S., minister in Mabou and at Port Hood, Cape Breton Island, from 1821 until his death on 16 November 1861. [HPC]

MILLER, Captain, master of the brig Isabella of Irvine from Troon bound for Quebec and Montreal in April 1833. [Times.15146]

MILLIGAN, ANDREW, in Milnton of Orr, testament 1793, Comm. Dumfries. [NRS]

MILLIGAN, ANDREW, a watchmaker, was admitted as a burgess and freeman of Ayr on 10 September 1800. [ABR]

MILLIGAN, DAVID, of Dalskairth, Troqueer, formerly a merchant in London, testament 1799, Comm. Dumfries. [NRS]

MILLIGAN, ELIZABETH, born 1747 in the Stewartry of Kirkcudbright, died in Pictou, Nova Scotia, on 28 February 1820. [AR.11.3.1820]

MILLIGAN, HUGH, born 1826, died 11 October 1896, husband of Jane, born 1824, died 4 January 1867, parents of Robert Milligan, born 1852, died in Joadja, New South Wales, Australia, on 18 December 1885, also Hugh Milligan, born 1854, died in Australia on 8 July 1916. [Ballantrae gravestone, Ayrshire]

MILLIGAN, JOHN, born 1774, an architect from Dumfries, emigrated to New Brunswick in 1820, died in St John, N.B., on 1 May 1821. [CG.2.5.1821]

MILLIGAN, MARY, in Carswadda, widow of James Milligan in Craigend, testament 1793, Comm. Dumfries. [NRS]

MILLIGAN, ROBERT, in Turnfine of Hills, Lochrutton, testament 1792, Comm. Dumfries. [NRS]

MILLIGAN, ROBERT, son of Thomas Milligan, [1785-1857], a plumber in Dumfries, and his wife Alison Wight Anderson, died in New York aged 37. [Dumfries gravestone]

MILLIGAN, WILLIAM, in the Kirkgate of Dumfries, testament 1795, Comm. Dumfries. [NRS]

MILLIGAN, WILLIAM, probably from Kirkbean, Kirkcudbrightshire, settled in South Carolina, died on Madeira in 1819. [NRS.CS46.1834.150]

MILROY, WILLIAM, born 1784, son of John Milroy, town clerk of Whithorn, and his wife Janet McMillan, died in Dominica on 3 June 1804. [Whithorn gravestone, Wigtownshire]

MITCHELL, ALEXANDER, from Ayr, a surgeon in Shepardston, Jefferson County, America, husband of Elizabeth Kearney, parents of John Mitchell born 1793. [SG.32.3]

MITCHELL, ALEXANDER, MD, son of John Mitchell an Exciseman in Ayr, died in Bladensburg, America, on 29 September 1804. [GM.75.1831]

MITCHELL, ALEXANDER, a country wright in Waterside of Fenwick, Ayrshire, accused of procuring an abortion by drugs in 1842. [NRS.AC14.42.95]

MITCHELL, or JOHNSTON, ANN, sister and heir of Thomas Mitchell in Phillan's Well, Ayrshire, 1842. [NRS.S/H]

MITCHELL, JAMES, born 1800 in Kilmarnock, Ayrshire, a carpet weaver who emigrated via Greenock to America, was naturalised in New York on 18 March 1822. [NARA]

MITCHELL, JOHN, born 1770, son of David Mitchell of Kirkmoatland, Dumfries-shire, [1729-1780], and his wife Jean Richardson, died at Montego Bay, Jamaica, on 8 September 1794. [Dumfries gravestone]ITCHELL, MATTHEW, born 1785, 'late of Jamaica', died on 23 September 1846. [Stewarton gravestone, Ayrshire]

MITCHELL, THOMAS, born 1805 in Greenock, a mariner in Charleston, South Carolina, was naturalised in S.C. on 29 September 1827. [NARA.M1183.1]

MOLLONS, ……., master of the Bella of Annan trading with Ulverstone in 1823. [NRS.E504.9.10]

MONIES, HUGH, born 1791 in Galloway, a resident of Charleston, South Carolina, was admitted as a citizen of S.C. on 19 October 1813. [NARA.M1183.1]

MONIES, JAMES, born 1776, a mariner from Kirkcudbright, was admitted as a citizen of South Carolina on 23 July 1804. [NARA.M1183.1]

MONCRIEFF, ROBERT LAIDLAW, born 1797, son of Reverend William Moncrieff and his wife Jean Laidlaw in Annan, Dumfries-shire, died at Harker's Hall, Jamaica, on 8 September 1836. [Annan gravestone]

MONTEATH, WILLIAM, born 5 November 1769 in Houston, Renfrewshire, son of Reverend John Monteath and his wife Anne Fullerton, a surgeon who died on St Vincent on 16 August 1793. [F.3.140] [Car.4.17]

MONTGOMERY, CHARLES, who 'after 35 years in Jamaica returned home aboard the Garthland, died in the Buck's Head Inn in Greenock in February 1804. [AJ.2928]

MONTGOMERIE, HUGH, son of Hament, 1801, Cough Montgomerie of Blackhouse in Ayrshire, died in Trinidad in 1822. [RAF]

MONTGOMERIE, JAMES, a merchant in New York, later in Haugh, parish of Urr, testament, 1801, Comm. Dumfries. [NRS]

MONTGOMERIE, JOHN, son of John Montgomerie and his wife Marion Paterson in Ardrossan, Ayrshire, settled in Trinidad, husband of Bethia Edmonstone, parents of Hugh Montgomerie, born there in 1822, John died in New York in 1830. [RAF][HAF]

MONTGOMERIE, JOHN, in 13 Cotton Street, Paisley, applied to settle in Canada on 2 May 1827. [TNA.CO384.5.991]

MONTGOMERIE, JOHN, in 35 Storie Street, Paisley, a member of the Paisley Emigration Society, applied to settle in Canada on 16 April 1827. [TNA.CO384.5.975]

MONTGOMERIE, ROBERT, son of Patrick Montgomerie of Blackhouse in Ayrshire, a merchant in Sevilla, Trinidad, around 1800. [RAF]

MONTGOMERY, ROBERT, from Irvine, Ayrshire, a merchant in St Croix, Danish West Indies, before 1829. [NRS.CS239.S49.9]; cf Robert Montgomery, in St Thomas, DWI, testament, 1824. [NRS.CS70.1.31]

MONTGOMERIE, THOMAS, third son of Alexander Montgomerie of Coilsfield and his wife Lilias, died in Dumfries, Virginia, on 13 August 1793. [HCA]

MONTGOMERIE, WILLIAM EWING, son of John Montgomerie and his wife Marion Paterson in Ardrossan, settled in St Croix, Danish West Indies, married ..... MacPherson, died in the West Indies on 13 August 1835. [HFA]

MOORE, WILLIAM, a merchant in Dumfries, testament 1800, Comm. Dumfries. [NRS]

MORINE, JOHN, in Chapel, Dunscore, testament 1793, Comm. Dumfries. [NRS]

MORRIS, ALEXANDER, master of the <u>Trepalsey of Greenock</u>, from Greenock bound for Newfoundland in 1806. [NRS.E504.15.77]

MORRIS, JAMES, born 1798 in Paisley, son of Alexander Morris, emigrated to Canada in 1801, later a politician. [BCB]

MORRIS, JOHN, a fisherman in Largs, Ayrshire, in 1839. [NRS.CS271.282]

MORRIS, WILLIAM, born 31 October 186 in Paisley, emigrated with parents to Upper Canada in 1801, a merchant and public official there, died in Montreal, Quebec on 29 June 1858. [BCB]

MORRISON, DANIEL, a skipper in Greenock, testament, 1810, Comm. Glasgow. [NRS]

MORRISON, JAMES, a merchant in Jamaica, deceased, husband of Mary Allan, a sasine, 1791. [NRS.RS.Wigtown.283]

MORRISON, MARGARET, spouse of Robert Lamont in Kirkland, Kirkcudbrightshire, daughter and heir of William Morrison of Kirkland, in 1825. [NRS.CS237.H11.21]

MORTON, JOHN, born 1790, first postmaster of Riccarton, died 29 July 1864, husband of Martha Watson, born 1792, died 22 January 1881. [Riccarton gravestone, Ayrshire]

MOUNEY, PETER, a labourer in Saltcoats, Ayrshire, was accused of rape in April 1817, trial papers. [NRS.JC26.1817.225]

MOUNSEY, ALEXANDER, from Dumfries-shire, then in Vaughan township, York County, Upper Canada, a petition, 1861. NLS.ms193]

MUIR, ALEXANDER, and Ann Bone, both born in Ayrshire, were married in St John, New Brunswick, on 9 March 1825. [NBC.12.3.1825]

MUIR, FREELAND, son of Andrew Muir, a merchant in Kirkcudbright, and his wife Anne Blair, died in St Vincent in June 1797. [AJ.2609]

MUIR, JAMES, born 12 April 1757 in Cumnock, Ayrshire, son of Reverend George Muir, was educated at Glasgow University in 1776, a minister in Bermuda from 1782 to 1787, later in Virginia from 1789 to 1820, died in Alexandria, Virginia, on 8 August 1820. [F.7.661] [RGG.456]

MUIR, JAMES, died in Greenock, Renfrewshire, on 20 December 1834. [NBC,12.2.1835]

MUIR, JANET, daughter of James Muir in Rosebank, Greenock, Renfrewshire, married William Boyd Kinnear, the Recorder of St John, New Brunswick, in Glasgow on 6 December 1830. [NBRG.5.3.1831]

MUIR, Dr JOHN, in Antigua, was admitted as a burgess and guilds-brother of Ayr on 2 October 1790. [ABR]

MUIR, ROBERT, master of the Hope of Ayr from Ayr to Pictou, Nova Scotia, in 1806. [NRS.E504.4.11]

MUIR, WILLIAM, born 1754 in Kirkcudbright, emigrated to New York in 1774, died 9 February 1809. [BAF]

MULLINGS, JOHN, born 1791 in Greenock, a pilot in Charleston, South Carolina, was naturalised in S.C. on 5 July 1824. [NARA.M1183.1]

MUNDELL, ALEXANDER, schoolmaster at Closeburn, residing at Wallace Hall, testament 1792, Comm. Dumfries. [NRS]

MUNRO, ANDREW, born 1794 in Dumfries, emigrated to Jamaica in 1818, died there on 18 December 1841. [Scots cemetery, Kingston, Jamaica]

MURDOCH, ALEXANDER, master of the Jane of Ayr from Greenock to Quebec in 1816, 1818, 1819, and 1820. [NRS.E504.15.111/119/125/128]

MURRAY, ARCHIBALD MURRAY, born 1826 in Ayrshire, son of James Murray a farmer, was educated at Glasgow University, later a minister in British Guiana from 1852 until his death on 3 December 1863. [F.7.674]

MURRAY, HENRY WILLIAM, son of John Dalrymple Murray of Murraythwaite, settled at the Holmes, Wellington, New Zealand, before 1853. [NRS.GD219.306]

MURRAY, JOHN CLARK, emigrated from Paisley to Quebec in 1862. [NRS.NRAS.1459/Acc.611/2]

MURRAY, WILLIAM, born 1784, son of Alexander Murray and his wife Catharine McGuffie, died in Jamaica on 22 August 1800. [Wigtown gravestone]

NAIRNE, J. G., messenger at arms, Castle Douglas, Kirkcudbrightshire, 1849. [POD]

NAIRNE, JOHN, in Causeway Street, Paisley, a victim of theft in 1831. [NRS.AD14.31.182]

NAIRN, THOMAS, tidesman at the port of Dumfries, testament 1795, Comm. Dumfries. [NRS]

NAIRN, WILLIAM, a smith in Bankend, testament 1799, Comm. Dumfries. [NRS]

NEIL, AGNES, widow of Archibald Lamont a labourer in Ardrossan, Ayrshire, a prisoner in Ayr Tolbooth accused of child murder in 1820. [NRS.JC26.1820.129]

NEIL, JAMES, master of the Neptune of Ayr from Greenock to Quebec in 1802, 1812, 1813, 1814, 1815, 1816, 1817, 1817; master of the Caledonia of Irvine from Greenock to Montreal, Quebec, in 1817. [NRS.E504.15.96/99/103/107/111/115/117]

NEIL, JOHN, master of the Robert of Irvine from Greenock to Quebec in 1817, 1818, 1819, 1820, 1821. [NRS.E504.15.119/122/ 125/ 128/135]

NEILSON, ISABELLA, eldest daughter of Reverend Neilson in Kirkbean, Kirkcudbrightshire, married Gilbert Sinclair, MD, from Jamaica, in Kirkbean Manse in 1813. [EA.5214.391]

NEILSON, JOHN, born in Dornald, Balmaghie, Kirkcudbrightshire, sixth child of William Neilson and his wife Isobel Brown, emigrated to Canada around 1790, editor of the Quebec Gazette, also a politician, died at Cap Rouge, Quebec on 1 February 1843. [BCB][Balmaghie gravestone]

NEILSON, NATHANIEL, of Springfield, born 1760, '25 years in Jamaica', died on 1 October 1834. [Buittle gravestone, Wigtownshire]

NEILSON, WILLIAM, master of the John and Jean of Ayr trading with Belfast in 1818. [NRS.E504.4.14]

NEILSON, WILLIAM, born 22 September 1772, son of William Neilson, 'an advocate for civil and religious liberty in America', died on 8 May 1857. [Balmaghie gravestone, Kirkcudbrightshire]

NELSON, EDWARD, born 1815 in Annan, Dumfries-shire, son of Benjamin Nelson and his wife Christian Irving Forrest, died in Heidelberg, Germany, on 21 April 1837. Annan gravestone]

NEWMAN, EBENEZER, a skipper in Greenock, testament, 1823, Comm. Glasgow. [NRS]

NICOL, JAMES, born 1798 in Paisley, Renfrewshire, emigrated via Greenock to America, was naturalised in New York on 27 November 1822. [NARA]

NICOL, ROBERT, a mariner in Irvine, Ayrshire, testament, 1813, Comm. Glasgow. [NRS]

NICHOLSON, JAMES, born 1782, died in Miramachi, New Brunswick, on 4 September 1848. [Dumfries gravestone]

NICOLSON, Dr THOMAS, born 1799 in Dumfries-shire, married Mary Paterson from Thornhill, Dumfries-shire, in 1818, a ship's surgeon from 1819 until 1822, settled in St John's, Antigua, in 1822, died on 8 July 1877. [Car.2.287]

NIVEN, JOHN, a staymaker, son of Hugh Niven a mason burgess of Ayr, was admitted as a burgess and guilds-brother of Ayr on 17 September 1800. [ABR]

NOBLE, GEORGE, married Geils Donald a daughter of Andrew Donald in Virginia, in Greenock on 18 September 1821. [EEC.17217]

NOBLE, JAMES, born in Mauchline, Ayrshire, a merchant partner of Noble and Arbuthnott in Norfolk, Virginia, died on 30 May 1810. [EA.4869]

ORR, GEORGE, born 1823, a gardener in Ayrshire, landed in Hobart, Tasmania, Australia, from the Sultana on 12 January 1856. [SRA.TD292]

ORR, HUGH, a merchant in Albany, New York, later in Kilbirnie, Ayrshire, testament, 10 March 1790, Comm. Glasgow. [NRS]

ORR, JAMES, a barber, son of William Orr a riding officer, was admitted as a burgess and guilds-brother of Ayr on 24 September 1800. [ABR]

ORR, JOHN, born 1830, a clerk from Ayrshire, landed in Hobart, Tasmania, Australia, from the Conway on 14 October 1855. [SRA.TD292]

ORR, WILLIAM, master of the Nared of Greenock, testament, 1817, Comm. Glasgow. [NRS]

OSBOURN, JOHN, born 1779, a tailor in Riccarton, died 5 October 1837. [Riccarton gravestone, Ayrshire]

OUGHTERSON, ARTHUR, a merchant in Barbados, later in Greenock, testament, 1817, Comm. Glasgow/ [NRS]

OUGHTERSON, JOHN, of Milnthird, a resident of Dumfries, testament 1799, Comm. Dumfries. [NRS]

PAGAN, Mrs JANE, born 1801 in Moffat, Dumfries-shire, emigrated to Canada in 1821, widow of J. Pagan, died in Pictou, Nova Scotia, on 25 May 1831. [HJ.20.6.1831]

PAISLEY, ROBERT, born 1812, a labourer in Kirkmahoe, Dumfries-shire, accused of poaching in 1832. [NRS.AD14.32.81]

PARK, BREDDIE, born 1784 in Greenock, died in Jamaica on 20 June 1811. [Kingston Cathedral gravestone, Jamaica]

PARKER, WILLIAM, born 11 January 1804 in Kilmarnock, Ayrshire, son of William Parker and his wife Agnes Paterson, a Lieutenant of the Bengal Army, died in Cawnpore, India, on 10 April 1831. [BA.3.459]

PATERSON, ALEXANDER, agent in Irvine, Ayrshire, for the Union Bank of Scotland in 1849. [POD]

PATERSON, JAMES, in Clarkhill, testament 1792, Comm. Dumfries. [NRS]

PATERSON, JAMES, a skipper in Greenock, testament, 1812, Comm. Glasgow. [NRS]

PATTERSON, JAMES, a mason in Lockerbie, Dumfries-shire, emigrated to Halifax, Nova Scotia, in 1815, father of James Patterson, born 4 March 1816 in Torthorwald, Dumfries-shire. [Torthorwald gravestone]

PATERSON, JAMES, in 9 Abbey Street, Paisley, applied to settle in Canada on 2 March 1827. [TNA.CO384.5.1011]

PATERSON, JOHN, master of the Jessies of Ayr from Greenock to Montreal and Quebec in 1796. [NRS.E504.15.71]

PATTERSON, JOHN, born in Galloway, died in Halifax, Nova Scotia, on 20 May 1827. [AR.26.5.1827]

PATTERSON, ROBERT, born 1732 in Renfrew, emigrated to America in 1763, settled in Churchville, Maryland, in 1767, a surveyor, vis Philadelphia, Pennsylvania, to Pictou, Nova Scotia, aboard the Betsey in 1768, died there on 30 September 1808. [DCB][SF]

PATERSON, WALTER, a shopkeeper at Keirmiln, testament 1793, Comm. Dumfries. [NRS], testament, 1790, Comm. Glasgow. [NRS]

PATERSON, WALTER, born 1798, son of Walter Paterson, [1762-1840], and his wife Elizabeth Hannah, [1762-1837], died in Jamaica in 1826. [Buittle gravestone, Kirkcudbrightshire]

PATERSON, WILLIAM, born 1755 in Kilmarnock, Ayrshire, 'late of Jamaica', died in Wellington Square, Ayr on 9 June 1832. [Kilmarnock, Laigh, gravestone] [AJ.4407]

PATTERSON, WILLIAM, son of Reverend Henry Patterson in Gateside, Dumfries-shire, died in Antigua on 18 July 1843. [EEC.20650]

PATON, HUGH, born 1775, a vintner in Kilmarnock, Ayrshire, died in March 1834, husband of Jean ......, born 1783, died 12 October 1844. [Riccarton gravestone, Ayrshire]

PATRICK, D., agent of the Union Bank of Scotland in Dalry, Ayrshire, in 1849. [POD]

PATRICK, JOHN, second son of John Patrick in Trearne, Ayrshire, was educated at Glasgow University in 1783, [MAGU], married Sarah Ann Stewart in New York on 6 December 1801, [SM.64.180]; he died in New York on 31 October 1827. [BM.21.120]

PATRICK, ROBERT, son of James Patrick of Drumbuie in Ayrshire, and his wife Anne Shedden, a merchant in Bermuda, died in 1809. [RAF]

PATRICK, WILLIAM, son of James Patrick of Drumbuie in Ayrshire, and his wife Anne Shedden, a merchant in Virginia around 1800. [RAF]

PATTEN, THOMAS, a merchant in St John's, Newfoundland, also a shipowner in Greenock in 1806. [NRS.CE60.11.8/10]

PATTIE, JOHN, in Lucea, Hanover, Jamaica, later in Park of Troquier, testament, 1816, Comm. Dumfries. [NTS]

PATTISON, ALEXANDER, a manufacturer and bleacher, formerly in Paisley, Renfrewshire, later in Neilston, Renfrewshire.

PATTON, GEORGE, born 1749 in Paisley, 'a resident of New Providence for 20 years', died on 22 October 1807. [Bahamas Royal Gazette, 24.10.1807]

PATON, JOHN, born 1798, a merchant from Greenock, settled at Orange Hill, Montego Bay, St James, Jamaica, on 21 May 1841. [Montego Bay gravestone]

PAUL, JOHN, from Charleston, South Carolina, married Isabella Kerr MacWhinnie, second daughter of William MacWhinnie a merchant, in Kirkcudbright on 27 July 1829. [BM.26.841]

PAUL, ROBERT, in Lochmaben, testament 1793, Comm. Dumfries. [NRS]

PAXTON, GEORGE, in Richardland, born 1780, died 15 January 1856, husband of Isabella Carse, born 1791, died 21 December 1831. [Riccarton gravestone, Ayrshire]

PEACOCK, HUGH, a butcher in Girvan, Ayrshire, testaments, 1793-1808, Comm. Glasgow. [NRS]

PEACOCK, ROBERT, born 1796 in Paisley, died in Lubeck, Germany, on 2 March 1880. [EC.29779]

PEDDIE, Mrs AGNES, daughter of James Peddie of Ruchill, testament, 1793, Comm. Glasgow. [NRS]

PEDEN, GAVIN, born 1770, Quartermaster of the 2nd Dragoons, died 19 April 1825, husband of Isabella Meikle. [Riccarton gravestone, Ayrshire]

PEEBLES, JAMES, son of Reverend William Peebles in Newtown-on-Ayr, Ayrshire, graduated MA from Glasgow University in 1801, settled in Kingston, Jamaica, died there on 23 June 1822. [MAGU][S.294.285] [EEC.17347]

PEIL, JOHN, a chaise driver in Dumfries, testament, 1792, Comm. Dumfries. [NRS]

PETER, CATHERINE, daughter of James Peter in Gourock, married A. G. Berry, son of William Berry in Jamaica, in Glasgow on 11 July 1861.

PHILIPSON, MICHAEL, an innkeeper in Dumfries, testament, 1790, Comm. Dumfries. [NRS]

PICKEN, ANDREW, born in Stewarton, Ayrshire, emigrated to New York aboard the New York on 3 October 1785, died 1796. [ANY]

PICKEN, ANDREW, born 1802 in Paisley, Renfrewshire, son of Ebenezer Picken, a teacher in the West Indies from 1822 to 1828, emigrated to America in 1830, died in Montreal, Quebec, in 1849. [TSA]

PICKERING, JOSEPH, in Dumfries, a victim of crime in 1842. [NRS.AD14.42.407]

POLLOCK, DAVID, tenant in Nether Place, testament, 1791, Comm. Glasgow. [NRS]

POLLOCK, GEORGE, a merchant in Paisley, Renfrewshire, testament, 1796, Comm. Glasgow. [NRS]

POLLOCK, JEAN, in Common Loan of Paisley, Renfrewshire, testament, 1800, Comm. Glasgow. [NRS]

POLLOCK, JOHN, a merchant on the James River, Virginia, eldest son of John Pollock portioner of Overton of Achenbothieblair, Lochwinnoch, Renfrewshire, 1800, 1801. [NRS.CS17.1.19/123; CS17.1.9/112; CS18.18.708.4]

POLLOCK, THOMAS, a merchant in Paisley, Renfrewshire, father of George Pollock in Boston, USA, probate November 1838, PCC. [TNA]

POOL, GEORGE, master of the sloop Countess Mansfield of Annan, trading with Ulverston in 1823. [NRS.E504.9.10]; testament, 1825, Comm. Dumfries. [NRS]

PORTEOUS, JOHN, son of Robert Porteous a baillie of Dumfries, died in Kingston, Jamaica on 28 December 1807. [SM.70.317]

PORTER, DAVID KENNEDY, born 1840, died in Allahabad in the East Indies on 2 October 1859, son of John Porter, [1812-1871], and his wife Hannah Gemmel. [Riccarton gravestone, Ayrshire]

PORTER, WILLIAM, a shipmaster in Saltcoats, Ayrshire, testament, 1791, Comm. Glasgow. [NRS]

POTTER, MARGARET, daughter of Captain George Potter in Greenock, married John Ellis from Prince Edward Island, in Liverpool, England, on 4 October 1848. [SG.1757]

POTTS, JOHN, from Dumfries, died at Ballard's River, Clarendon, Jamaica, on 15 February 1798. [AJ.2635]

POTT, WILLIAM, in Netherton of Carswadda, Lochrutton, testament, 1793, Comm. Dumfries. [NRS]

PRIDE, Captain, master of the Mary Ann of Greenock from Glasgow bound for St John, New Brunswick, in 1859. [BSL.IX.46]

PURSAL, JOHN, an Anti-Burgher and a travelling merchant, was admitted as a burgess and guild-brother of Ayr on 23 March 1818. [ABR]

PURCELL, JOHN, a skipper in Greenock, testament, 1806, Comm. Glasgow. [NRS]

RAE, GEORGE, formerly in Virginia, later in Dumfries by 1793. [NRS.CS17.1.12/378]

RAE, JAMES, a skipper in Greenock, testament, 1812, Comm. Glasgow. [NRS]

RAE, JOHN, born 1776 in Dumfries-shire, emigrated with his wife and seven children to Canada in 1834, a school superintendent in Nappan, Nova Scotia, died there on 13 October 1834. [NBC.15.11.1834]

RAE, WILLIAM, in Durrisdeer, testament, 1795, Comm. Dumfries. [NRS]

RAE, WILLIAM, born 1762 in Dumfries, settled in Jamaica in 1782, died in Kingston, Jamaica, on 7 May 1837. [Scots cemetery gravestone]

RAE, WILLIAM, a farmer in Durrisdeer, Dumfries-shire, a decreet, 1830. [NRS.CS46.1830.155]

RAE, ……, master of the Martha of Dumfries trading with Beaumaris, Anglesay, Wales, in 1823. [NRS.E504.9.10]

RAFFELL, WILLIAM, in Carsethorn, testament, 1793, Comm. Dumfries. [NRS]

RAIN, GEORGE, of the Crown Inn, Castle Douglas, Kelton, Dumfries-shire, was a victim of forgery and theft in 1850. [NRS.AD14,50.521]

RAMSAY, ALEXANDER, a spirit dealer, formerly in Glasgow, lately in Stewarton, Ayrshire, testament, 1800, Comm. Glasgow. [NRS]

RAMSAY, GRIZEL, relict of Robert Sinclair a shipmaster in Crawfordsdyke, Renfrewshire, testament, 1792, Comm. Glasgow. [NRS]

RAMSAY, ROBERT, fourth son of Robert Ramsay a writer in Dumfries, died in Surinam on 24 April 1818. [BM.3.248]

RAMSAY, ROBERT, from Maybole, Ayrshire, settled as a wright in Baltimore, Maryland, by 1819. [NRS.CS17.1.38/528]

RAMSAY, ROBERT, born 1820, died in Port Henry, Australia, on 17 January 1855. [Greenock gravestone]

RAMSAY, THOMAS KENNEDY, born 7 January 1788, son of Reverend John Ramsay and his wife Margaret McFadzean, a Lieutenant of the 11th Bengal Native Infantry, died at Komona on 30 October 1807. [BA.3.606]

RAMSAY, WILLIAM, in the Townhead of Ayr, testament, 1792, Comm. Glasgow. [NRS]

RAMSAY, ..., son of Robert Ramsay, [1739-1810], and his wife Jean Malcolm, [1740-1820], died in New Providence in the Bahama Islands aged 3. [Dumfries gravestone]

RANALDSON, JOHN, of Blairhall, residing in Youngfield, testament, 1797, Comm. Dumfries. [NRS]

RANKIN, ALAN, from Bridge of Weir, Renfrewshire, bound via Quebec to settle in Upper Canada in 1820. [NRS.SC58.75.79]

RANKIN, JANE, eldest daughter of John Rankin, a merchant in Greenock, Renfrewshire, married Hinton Spalding, MD, of New Grange, Jamaica, in Greenock on 2 April 1811. [SM.73.317]

RANKIN, JOHN, formerly a merchant in Barbados, died at Prospect Hill, Largs, Ayrshire, on 17 March 1829

REA, JAMES SIMPSON, son of John Harvey in Castle Semple, died at Crayfish Estate, Grenada, on 4 June 1829. [BM.26.411]

REAY, JOHN, born in Dalmellington, Ayrshire, died in Roseau, Dominica, on 24 April 1821. [BM.10.359] [EEC.17214] [S.4.246]

REED, JAMES, eldest son of James Reed, MD, in Kilmarnock, Ayrshire, died in New Orleans, Louisiana, on 18 September 1839. [SG.821]

REID, ANDREW, at Kilbirnie Bridge, Ayrshire, son of Andrew Reid a mariner there, youngest son of William Reid a weaver in Kilbirnie, testaments, 1792, Comm. Glasgow. [NRS]

REID, DAVID, master of the <u>Trelawney</u>, testament, 1819, Comm. Glasgow. [NRS]

REID, DAVID, born 28 August 1813, son of James Reid and his wife Helena, a Major General of the Bengal Army, died on 29 February 1876. [BA.3.626]

REID, FRANCIS, born 1788, son of James Reid and his wife Ann Halliday in Dalton, Dumfries-shire, a surgeon of the 35th Regiment of Foot, died on St Lucia on 5 April 1828. [Dalton gravestone]

REID, GEORGE, a timber merchant in Johnstone, Renfrewshire, testament, 1791, Comm. Glasgow. [NRS]

REID, GEORGE, a merchant in Port Glasgow, later at Bridge of Johnstone, Renfrewshire, testaments, 1791, Comm. Glasgow. [NRS]

REID, JAMES, master of the Caledonia of Irvine from Greenock bound for Montreal in 1816; master of the True Briton of Irvine from Greenock bound for Montreal, Quebec in 1820 and 1821. [NRS.E504.15.112/128/135]

REID, JOHN, from Dumfries, a merchant in Norfolk, Virginia, died on 29 October 1791. [AM.53.568].37]

REID, JOHN, a merchant in Virginia, died in London on 13 November 1791, son of James Reid in Dumfries. [GCr.37]

REID, JOHN, born 1757, son of Matthew Reid and his wife Mary Irving in Dornock, Dumfries-shire, died in Jamaica, on 25 December 1816. [Dornock gravestone]

REID, JOHN, master of the Howarden Castle of Ayr from Greenock to Pictou, Nova Scotia, in 1818. [NRS.E504.15.120]

REID, JOHN, agent in Johnstone, Renfrewshire, for the City of Glasgow Bank in 1849. [POD]

REID, THOMAS, a weaver in Caerlaverock, testament, 1792, Comm. Dumfries. [NRS]

REID, THOMAS, a merchant in Stevenston, later in Saltcoats, Ayrshire, testaments, 1789-1790, Comm. Glasgow. [NRS]

REID, WILLIAM, in Johnstone, Renfrewshire, applied to settle in Canada on 28 February 1815. [NRS.RH9]

REID, Reverend WILLIAM, born 27 March 1811 in Paisley, Renfrewshire, son of Robert Reid a merchant, a minister in Gretna, Dumfries-shire, died in Huntly, Mandeville, Jamaica, on 25 October 1866. [F.2.397]

RENFREW, ROBERT, a merchant in New York, heir to his father Robert Renfrew a smith in Paisley, Renfrewshire, who died 14 November 1831. [NRS.S/H]

RENNIE, DAVID, a merchant in St John's, Newfoundland, and a shipowner in Greenock, 1801. [NRS.CE60.11.5/28; 7/12/15]

RENWICK, JAMES, born 1744 in Lochmaben, Dumfries-shire, married Catharine Mee in 1768, emigrated via England to New York in 1783, a merchant there, died 25 September 1803. [ANY]

REOCH, ROBERT, a colour-maker in Riverpoint, Rhode Island, heir to Bethia Tennant, widow of Robert Reoch a calico printer in Grahamston, Renfrewshire, 1875. [NRS.S/H]

RIALL, Major General, Governor of Grenada, married Elizabeth Scarlett, daughter of James Scarlett jr of Peru, Jamaica, in Senwick, Kirkcudbrightshire, on 19 December 1819. [BM.6.606]

RICHARDS, Captain ARTHUR, born 1784, of the Queensberry Arms Inn in Annan, Dumfries-shire, died in the West Indies in December 1823. [SM.93.128]

RICHARDSON, GABRIEL, son of Gabriel Richardson a brewer in Dumfries, was apprenticed for six years to John Ballantyne, a cooper in Edinburgh, on 27 March 1800. [ERA]

RICHARDSON, JAMES, from Carruthers, Mousewold Mains, Dumfries-shire, died in Clarendon, Jamaica, on 12 August 1811. [DPCA.488]

RICHARDSON, JOHN, in Heck or Dubside, Lochmaben, Dumfries-shire, was he victim of assault in 1830. [NRS.AD14.30.149]

RICHARDSON, WILLIAM, in America, nephew and heir of Mathew Richardson in Guileburn, Dumfries-shire, who died 19 January 1846. [NRS.S/H]

RICHARDSON, WILLIAM, agent in Lockerbie, Dumfries-shire, for the Western Bank of Scotland in 1849. [POD]

RIDDELL, ALEXANDER, from Virginia, later in Dumfries by 1799. [NRS.CS17.1.18/189]

RIDDELL, DOROTHY, second daughter of Thomas Riddell of Swinburn Castle, Northumberland, a resident of Dumfries, testament, 1796, Comm. Dumfries. [NRS]

RIDDELL, JEAN, daughter of Robert Riddell of Glenriddell, testament, 1792, Comm. Dumfries. [NRS]

RIDDELL, WAUCHOPE, in Dumfries, daughter of Robert Riddell of Glenriddell, testament, 1792, Comm. Dumfries. [NRS]

RIDDELL, or WAUCHOPE, Mrs, in Dumfries, daughter of Walter Riddell, testament, 1799, Comm. Dumfries. [NRS]

RIDDICK, ROBERT, of Corbiton, resident of Dumfries, testament, 1799, Comm. Dumfries. [NRS]

RISK, JOHN, agent in Paisley for the Western Bank of Scotland in 1849. [POD]

RITCHIE, ADAM, a farmer in Canada, son and heir of John Ritchie in Johnstone, Renfrewshire, 1838. [NRS.S/H]

RITCHIE, ALEXANDER, an Anti-Burgher and a grocer, was admitted as a burgess and guild-brother of Ayr on 23 September 1814. [ABR]

RITCHIE, ALEXANDER, born in Lochmaben, Dumfries-shire, a planter, died on Lochmaben Estate, Cedar Point, Trinidad, in 1822. [BM.12.885]

RITCHIE, DAVID, the younger, formerly a surgeon in the Service of the East India Company, later in Challoch House, near Stranraer, Wigtownshire, a deed, 1831. [NRS.GD3.1.9.6.24.12]

RITCHIE, JOHN, a traveller in Montreal, Quebec, son and heir of Jessie Robertson, wife of William Ritchie a manufacturer in Ayr, who died 22 December 1856. [NRS.S/H]

RITCHIE, MARGARET, wife of James Ronald a cabinet-maker in America, heir to he brother William Ritchie a sailor in Irvine, Ayrshire. 1807. [NRS.S/H]

RITCHIE, THOMAS, a merchant from Greenock, Renfrewshire, died in Barbados in March 1813. [Barbados Mercury, 9.3.1813][EA.5156.13]

RITCHIE, WILLIAM, master of the <u>Corsair of Greenock</u> from Greenock bound for Quebec and Montreal, in 1834, 1835, 1836, 1837, with passengers, from Tobermory, Mull, with passengers bound for Cape Breton and Quebec in 1838. [QM][GA]

ROAN, JOHN, in Barhead, Orchardton, Renwick, Kirkcudbrightshire, a victim of theft in 1824. [NRS.AD14.24.150]

ROBERTSON, Reverend ANDREW, married Jane McLatchie, daughter of William McLatchie in Tobago, in Greenock, Renfrewshire, on 26 March 1827. [EA.6609.207]

ROBERTSON, DANIEL, in San Francisco, California, son and heir of John Robertson a weaver in Paisley, Renfrewshire, who died 21 October 1873. [NRS.S/H]

ROBERTSON, DAVID, a currier in Dumfries, testament, 1790, Comm. Dumfries. [NRS]

ROBERTSON, Reverend FREDERICK, in Greenock, Renfrewshire, father of Charles Lachlan Robertson born 29 July 1861, a minister in Canada and the USA. [F.3.435]

ROBERTSON, HELEN, daughter of Archibald Robertson in Greenock, married Arthur Oughterson from Barbados on 18 November 1817. [BM.2.358]

ROBERTSON, JAMES, in Cummertrees, testament, 1793, Comm. Dumfries. [NRS]

ROBERTSON, JAMES, eldest son of John Robertson a thread manufacturer in Paisley, Renfrewshire, settled in Sussex, New Jersey or Virginia, by 1796. [NRS.CS17.1.15/220; CS17.1.15/399; CS17.1.27/35]

ROBERTSON, JOHN, in Wellhalket, born 1742, died 22 May 1811, husband of Jean Muir, born 1756, died 20 February 1839. [Dunlop gravestone, Ayrshire]

ROBERTSON, JOHN, a sailor in Troon, Ayrshire, testament, 1807, Comm. Glasgow. [NRS]

ROBERTSON, JOHN, born 1815 in Greenock, Renfrewshire, a carpenter in the Swan River Colony, Western Australia, by 1830, husband of Christian ....., born in Greenock. [BPP.3.444]

ROBERTSON, PETER, a merchant in Belleville, Canada, son and heir of David Robertson a minister in Kilmaurs, Ayrshire, who died on 10 June 1846. [NRS.S/H]

ROBERTSON, ROBERT, born 1798, a cheese dealer, died 27 March 1887, husband of Jean Howie, born 1806, died 16 June 1888. [Dunlop gravestone, Ayrshire]

ROBERTSO, WILLIAM, a merchant in Greenock, via Liverpool to America in 1801. [NRS.CS17.1.2/467]

ROBERTSON, WILLIAM, from Renfrew, a merchant in Yarmouth, Shelbourne, Nova Scotia, in 1803, 1809. [NRS.SC58.61.21; CS17.1.28/320]

ROBERTSON, WILLIAM, a skipper in Greenock, later in Fairlie, Ayrshire, testament, 1808, Comm. Glasgow. [NRS]

ROBERTSON, WILLIAM, master of the Trim of Greenock from Greenock bound for Newfoundland in 1815. [NRS.E504.15.109]

ROBINSON, DOUGLAS, born 24 November 1824 in Orchardton, Kirkcudbrightshire, son of George Rose Robertson, emigrated to Philadelphia, Pennsylvania, in 1842, later settled in Herkimmer County, New York, died at sea on board the Kaiser Wilhelm III on 25 November 1893. [ANY]

ROBISON, MARGARET, widow of George Bell of Conbeath, testament, 1792, Comm. Dumfries. [NRS]

ROBISON, WILLIAM, born 1763, died in Bergen Neck, New Jersey, on 24 January 1849. [Balmaghie gravestone, Kirkcudbrightshire]

ROBSON, JAMES, from Paisley, Renfrewshire, settled in New York by 1798. [NRS.CS17.1.17/12]

ROBSON, JAMES, portioner of Kirktoun, testament, 1800, Comm. Dumfries. [NRS]

ROBSON, JOHN, agent of the Edinburgh and Glasgow Bank in Dumfries, in 1849. [POD]

RODDICK, Reverend JAMES, and his wife Mary Dickson in Gretna, Dumfries-shire, were parents of James Roddick, born 28 May 1852, later a minister in Adelaide, South Australia. [F.2.248]

RODGER, ALEXANDER agent in Greenock, for the Clydesdale Bank in 1849. [POD]

RODGER, JAMES, a butcher, son of David Rodger a butcher burgess and guilds-brother, was admitted as a burgess and guilds-brother of Ayr on 24 September 1800. [ABR]

ROGERS, JOSEPH, born 1794 in Paisley, Renfrewshire, a stonecutter who emigrated via Greenock to America, was naturalised in New York on 19 February 1823. [NY Court of Common Pleas]

RODGER, WILLIAM, an assistant surgeon of the Royal Navy, son of deacon James Rodger in Ayr, died in Grenada in October 1838. [SG.769]

ROGERSON, JAMES, a merchant in St John's, Newfoundland, and a shipowner in Greenock, 1805, 1806. [NRS.CE60.11.8/15/14]

ROGERSON, SAMUEL, in St John's, Newfoundland, brother of William Rogerson in Gilliesbie, Lockerbie, Dumfries-shire, a letter, 24 September 1829. [NRS.GD1.620.95]

ROLLO, AMELIA, widow of William Irving of Bonshaw, testament, 1800, Comm. Dumfries. [NRS]

ROME, GEORGE, born 1773, from Langlands, Dornock, Dumfries-shire, '35 years in Trent Hills, Long Island', died in 1857. [AO]

ROME, GEORGE, born 1798, died at North Portland Avenue, Brooklyn, New York, on 15 May 1879. [AO]

ROME, GEORGE, from Annan, Dumfries-shire, married Margaret Paterson, daughter of Robert Paterson from Inverness, in Brooklyn, New York, on 15 March 1870. [AO]

ROME, HENRY B., born 1840, son of George Rome from Annan, Dumfries-shire, died in Brooklyn, New York, on 13 December 1872. [AO]

ROME, MARY ANN, born 1804, wife of George Rome, died in Wheatley, Long Island, New York, on 14 October 1861. [AO]

ROME, JAMES STEWART, born 1815, died in Havannah, Cuba, on 6 March 1833, [Dornock gravestone, Dumfries-shire]

ROME, TRISTRAM, in Langlands, Dornock, testament, 1795, Comm. Dumfries. [NRS]

ROME, TRISTRAM, born 1773, son of John Rome and his wife Jean Cockpen, settled in Dominica before 1795, died there in 1797. [Dornock gravestone]

ROME, Mrs, wife of G. D. Rome from Heathfield, Annan, Dumfries-shire, died at 184 Devoe Street, Williamsburgh, Long Island, New York, on 8 July 1876. [AO]

ROME, ..., master of the Neptune of Dumfries trading with Beaumaris, Wales, in 1825. [NRS.E504.9.10]

RONALDS, JAMES, born 1752 in Paisley, Renfrewshire, settled in America around 1776, a carpenter and builder in New York, died on 17 May 1812. [ANY]

ROPER, Captain, master of the Hound of Greenock from the Clyde bound for Newfoundland in 1853. [EEC]

RORISON, WILLIAM, a herd in Benbuie, testaments, 1798, Comm. Dumfries. [NRS]

ROSE, GEORGE, in Miramachi, New Brunswick, died in Summervale, Ayrshire, on 20 July 1827. [DPCA.1304]

ROSE, HAMILTON, agent of the Bank of Scotland in Cumnock, Ayrshire, in 1849. [POD]

ROSS, GEORGE CLARK, born 25 October 1798, died in Brompton, Canada East, on 1 November 1852. [Crossmichael gravestone, Dumfries-shire]

ROSS, HUGH, an innkeeper in Ballantrae, Ayrshire, imprisoned in Edinburgh, trial papers, 1818. [NRS.JC26.1818.82]; summons for wrongous imprisonment, 1818. [NRS.CS232.R15.17]

ROSS, JAMES, master of the Jane of Ayr from Greenock to Quebec in 1814. [NRS.E504.15.107]

ROSS, J. B., agent in Girvan, Ayrshire, for the Clydesdale Bank in 1849. [POD]

ROSS, THOMAS, master of the James Hamilton of Ardrossan from Greenock to Newfoundland in 1819. [NRS.E504.15.124]

ROSS, WILLIAM, a sailor in Girvan, Ayrshire, testament, 1808, Comm. Glasgow. [NRS]

ROSS, WILLIAM, born 26 October 1804, a mason on Loch Ryan Estate, died 26 December 1895, his wife Agnes died on 19 September 1898. [Cairnryan gravestone, Wigtownshire]

ROWAN, DAVID, an Anti-Burgher and a grocer, son of David Rowan in Miln Vennel, Ayr, a burgess and guilds-brother there, was admitted as a burgess and guild-brother of Ayr on 6 September 1804. [ABR]

ROWAND, JOHN, from Paisley, a merchant in Virginia in 1801. [NRS.CS17.1.9/383]

RUDDICK, GEORGE, a tenant farmer in Greenhillhead, Lockerbie, Dumfries-shire, was accused of assaulting John Richardson sr., in Heck or Dubbieside, Lochmaben, in 1830. [NRS.AD14.30.149]

RUDDICK, ..., master of the John and Mary of Kirkcudbright trading between Ulverston and Dumfries in 1825. [NRS.E504.9.10]

RUSSELL, WILLIAM, born 1764 or 1770 in Cumnock, Ayrshire, a merchant, applied to become a citizen of South Carolina, on 24 May 1804. [NARA.M1183.1]; died in Charleston, S.C., on 16 January 1815. [AJ.3258]

RUSSELL, WILLIAM, in Philadelphia, Pennsylvania, a letter to his brother John Russell in Moffat, Dumfries-shire, in 1822. [NRS.NRAS.1267, bundle 1]

RUTHERFORD, SAMUEL, a shoemaker in Townhead, Lockerbie, Dumfries-shire, was accused of assault in 1825. [NRS.AD14.25.232]

SAMSON, JAMES, second son of John Samson, a farmer in Finlayston, Ochiltree, Ayrshire, died in Spanish Town, Jamaica, in 1818. [S.68.18]

SAMSON, THOMAS, son of Thomas Samson, [1777-1856], died in St Croix, Danish West Indies. [Kilmarnock Laigh gravestone]

SAUNDERS, WILLIAM, from Closeburn, Dumfries, died in Trinidad in 1817. [S.22.17]

SCAMBLE, JOHN, born 1809, son of George Scamble, died in Trinidad on 27 July 1828. [Wigtown gravestone]

SCOBIE, ANDREW, in Bridge of Weir, Renfrewshire, bound via Quebec to settle in Upper Canada in 1820. [NRS.SC58.75.79]

SCOTLAND, WILLIAM, a shipmaster from Greenock, married Jessie Buchanan in London on 4 July 1860, their son Andrew Gibson Scott was born aboard the Saguenay in New York harbour on 22 September 1865. [NRS.NRH.MRB]

SCOTT, ANDREW, born in Paisley, died in Portland, America, in September 1818. [S.3.95]

SCOTT, or MCCALLUM, ANN H., in Quebec, heir of Janet Morrison, widow of Thomas Orr a skipper in Greenock, Renfrewshire, 1830. [NRS.S/H]

SCOTT, FRANCIS, in Backgreen, Middlebie, testaments, 1795/1796, Comm. Dumfries. [NRS]

SCOTT, HAMILTON, Captain, master of the Corsair of Greenock from Leith via Cromarty with passengers bound for Pictou, Nova Scotia, and Quebec, in 1831. [QM]

SCOTT, HELEN, born 1780, from Paisley, wife of George Carswell, died at Wing Lake, Bloomfield township, Oakland County, Michigan, on 28 August 1844. [SG.1342]

SCOTT, HUGH, born 1760, died 25 September 1815, husband of Marion McCallan, born 1768, died 24 July 1820, parents of James Scott, who settled in Montreal, Quebec. [Ballantrae gravestone]

SCOTT, JAMES, master of the Union of Greenock from Greenock bound for Pictou, Nova Scotia, in 1822. [NRS.E504.15.139]

SCOTT, JANET, from Annan, Dumfries-shire, married Andrew R. Rome a printer in Brooklyn, New York, in Jersey City, New Jersey, on 18 October 1864; she died in Brooklyn on 17 June 1865. [AO]

SCOTT, JOHN, a carter in Dumfries, testament, 1794, Comm. Dumfries. [NRS] in 1849. [POD]

SCOTT, JOHN, in Fredericksburg, America, brother and heir of Margaret Scott in Greenock, Renfrewshire, 1840. [NRS.S/H]

SCOTT, JOHN, agent in Paisley for the Union Bank of Scotland in 1849. [POD]

SCOTT, JOHN, in Canada West, brother and heir to James Scott a divinity student in Annan, Dumfries-shire, 1857. [NRS.S/H]

SCOTT, ROBERT, a mason in Langholm, Dumfries-shire, testament, 1797, Comm. Dumfries. [NRS]

SCOTT, ROBERT, from Hawick, Roxburghshire, a divinity student in 1825, settled in Canada. [AUPC]

SCOTT, THOMAS, in Jamaica, son and heir of John Scott in Flowerbank, Sanquhar, Dumfries-shire, 1839. [NRS.S/H]

SCOTT, WALTER, in Mavisbank, Kirkconnell, Dumfries-shire, testament, 1791, Comm. Dumfries. [NRS]

SCOTT, WILLIAM, son of James Scott in Langholm, Dumfries-shire, was apprenticed to Thomas Chalmers, a locksmith in Edinburgh, for six years. In 1797. [ERA]

SCOTT, WILLIAM, a former gunner of the Royal Artillery, with his wife and family in Becknows, Canonby, Langholm, Dumfries-shire, applied to settle in Canada on 1 March 1819. [TNA.CO384.5.793]

SCOTT, ……., master of the Blossom of Annan trading between Caernarvon and Dumfries in 1824. [NRS.E504.9.10]

SERVICE, Captain GEORGE, master of the Jean of Greenock, testament, 1808, Comm. Glasgow. [NRS]

SERVICE, THOMAS, born 1767 in Irvine, Ayrshire, a merchant in New York, married Sarah Tinney in 1796, died 21 November 1806. [ANY]

SETON, JOHN GORDON, a farmer in Quebec, nephew and heir of Sarah Seton, wife of William Robertson a dyer in Largs, Ayrshire, who died on 12 December 1838. [NRS.S/H]

SHANKS, JOHN, from Greenock, Renfrewshire, a crewman on the Anna was drowned on 8 May 1830. [NBC.22.5.1830]

SHANNON, ALEXANDER, in Carbondale, America, grandson and heir of James Thompson in Dalbeattie, Kirkcudbrightshire, who died in 1816. [NRS.S/H]

SHARP, ARCHIBALD CAMPBELL, born 1793, son of James Sharp and his wife Mary, died in Geelong, Australia, on 4 December 1884. [Woodside gravestone, Paisley]

SHARP, WILLIAM, a skipper in Saltcoats, Ayrshire, testament, 1812, Comm. Glasgow. [NRS]

SHAW, ALEXANDER, eldest son of Reverend James Shaw in Greenock, Renfrewshire, was educated at Glasgow University in 1766, died in Jamaica on 10 August 1804. [MAGU][Car.4.15] [SM.66.885]

SHAW, JAMES, born 10 December 1780 in Craigie, Ayrshire, son of Reverend Dr Andrew Shaw and his wife Mary Lymburner, [1741-1826], emigrated via Greenock to the Bahamas on 10 December 1798. [Kilmarnock Laigh gravestone]

SHAW, JOHN, born 1811 in Greenock, Renfrewshire, emigrated to America in 1827, settled in Rockingham, New Hampshire, was naturalised there in February 1839. [NARA]

SHAW, ROBERT, born 1793, son of Thomas Shaw, [1772-1822], and his wife Mary Nicholson, [1772-1842], in Lockerbie, Dumfries-shire, settled in USA before 1850. [Dryfesdale gravestone]

SHAW, WALTER, born 1841, son of Walter Shaw and his wife Mary Ann Nelson, died at Moonlight Creek, New Zealand, on 21 July 1868. [Girvan gravestone]

SHEDDEN, WILLIAM, of Roughwood, Ayrshire, a merchant in New York, died there on 13 November 1798. [AJ.2661][EWJ.2.5.5]

SHEDDEN, WILLIAM RALSTON, from Roughwood, Ayr, died in New York, probate, July 1852, PCC. [TNA]

SHENNAN, ANDREW, in Langlands, Dornock, Dumfries-shire, testament, 1799, Comm. Dumfries. [NRS]

SHERROT, HELEN, born 1800 in Ayr, died in White Bluff, Georgia, on 21 October 1814. [Savanna Republican, 27.10.1814]

SHEERWOOD, ABRAHAM, a thief and housebreaker in Ayr, was sentenced on 12 April 1793 to be transported to the colonies for life. [AJ.2363]

SHIELDS, JAMES, in Ayr, applied to settle in Canada on 4 March 1815. [NRS.RH9]

SHIRREFF, DAVID, agent for the Western Bank of Scotland in Gatehouse of Fleet in 1849. [POD]

SIME, JAMES, a carpenter on the Princess of Wales of Greenock, testament, 1802, Comm. Glasgow. [NRS]

SIMPSON, ALEXANDER, born 1804, son of John Simpson and his wife Mary Cowan in Johnstone parish, emigrated to New York, died at Niagara in 1833. [Johnstone gravestone, Dumfries-shire]

SIMPSON, ALEXANDER, late of Simpson and Kelso in Greenock, died in New Orleans, Louisiana, on 5 April 1849. [SG.1820]

SIMPSON, JAMES, a skipper in Greenock, testament, 1808, Comm. Glasgow. [NRS]

SIMPSON, JOHN, born 1769, son of James Simpson the minister at Eastwood, Renfrewshire, died in Halifax, Nova Scotia, on 16 January 1820. [AR.22.1.1820]

SIMPSON, MARY ANN, wife of John Adams a manufacturer in South Carolina, grand-daughter and heir of James Simpson a skipper in Greenock, Renfrewshire, 1857. [NRS.S/H]

SIMPSON, Captain, master of the Gleniffer of Greenock trading between Greenock and Quebec in 1838. [SG.7.699]

SINCLAIR, ALEXANDER, born in Murr, Ayrshire, in 1806, died on 20 January 1825. [Kingston Cathedral gravestone, Jamaica]

SINCLAIR, JOHN, from Carsebuie, now a planter in Faquier County, Virginia, grandson of John Sinclair a merchant in Newton Stewart, Wigtownshire, a sasine, 1801. [NRS.RS.Wigtown.617]

SINCLAIR, JOHN, agent of the British Linen Company in Castle Douglas, Dumfries-shire, in 1849. [POD]

SINCLAIR, ROBERT, a weaver in Paisley, imprisoned in Glasgow accused of theft in 1820. [NRS.AD14.20.19]

SLIMMON, ROBERT, born 1819 in Sanquhar, Dumfries-shire, settled in New York in 1840 as a merchant, died on 8 November 1870. [ANY]

SLOANE, or CARSON, JANE, a farmer in Respin, sister and heir of Alexander Sloane in New Orleans, Louisiana, later in Whithorn,

Wigtownshire, who died on 13 December 1835; also, sister and heir of Anthony Sloane in New Orleans, who died on 3 January 1844; and heir to her brother Peter Sloane in New Orleans who died on 18 May 1844. [NRS.S/H]

SLOANE, JOHN, born 1791 in Dumfries-shire, emigrated with his wife and four children to Canada in 1821, settled in Caverhill, Queensbury, York County, New Brunswick. [PANB]

SLOANE, or BROWN, MARY, in Garrarie, Kirkcudbrightshire, niece and heir of Alexander Sloane in New Orleans, Louisiana, later in Whithorn, Wigtownshire, who died on 13 December 1835; also, sister and heir of Anthony Sloane in New Orleans, who died on 3 January 1844; and heir to her brother Peter Sloane in New Orleans who died on 18 May 1844. [NRS.S/H]

SLOAN, WILLIAM JAMES, postmaster in Holland Landing, Canada West, son and heir to James Sloan an Excise officer in Stranraer, Wigtownshire, who died on 12 June 1807. [NRS.S/H]

SLOSS, ANDREW, born 1782, died in Aldons on 11 October 1847, husband of Elizabeth Weir, born 1790, died in Holmshea,d on 27 June 1873, parents of Joan Sloss born 1825, wife of David McCosh, who died in Hannibal, America on 12 July 1849, and Duncan Sloss, who died in California aged 45. [Colmonell gravestone, Ayrshire]

SLOSS, GILBERT, an ironmonger from Ayr, died in St Vincent on 7 February 1851. [W.1200]

SMILLIE, DAVID, a shipmaster in Halifax, Nova Scotia, later in Paisley, 1815. [NRS.SC58.5.227]

SMITH, ADAM FREER, born 1 June 1791 in Galston, Ayrshire, son of Reverend George Smith and his wife Marion Freer, a merchant in Calcutta, India. [F.3.40]

SMITH, ALEXANDER, a mariner in Greenock, testament, 1801, Comm. Glasgow. [NRS]

SMITH, ANDREW, born 1790, formerly a surgeon in Montreal, Quebec, died in Smithfield on 21 April 1824. [Riccarton gravestone, Ayrshire]

SMITH, ANDREW, son of Deacon Smith a tailor in Ayr, an agent in New York for McKnight and McIlwraith haberdashers in Ayr, in 1800. [NRS.CS29.178.42]

SMITH, ANDREW, second son of Reverend Smith of Paisley Abbey parish, was lost at sea in January 1828, on passage from St John's, Newfoundland, and Halifax, Nova Scotia. [BM.24.807]

SMITH, ANDREW COVENTRY, born 1808, son of Joseph Smith and his wife Margaret Clegg in Ruthwell, Dumfries-shire, died in Jamaica on 25 March 1831. [Ruthwell gravestone]

SMITH, ANTONY, in Ironhash, Colvend, Kirkcudbrightshire, testament, 1793, Comm. Dumfries. [NRS]

SMITH, ARCHIBALD, a weaver in Girvan, Ayrshire, was accused of mobbing and rioting in 1817. [NRS.JC26.1817.225]

SMITH, DAVID, a carter in Ayr, was accused of assault in April 1817. [NRS.JC26.1817.225]

SMITH, ELIZABETH, in Dumfries, daughter of Robert Smith and his wife Susanna McGeorge in Craig Loaning, Dumfries, testament, 1792, Comm. Dumfries. [NRS]

SMITH, FRANCIS, born 1768, son of William Smith and his wife Jean Currie in Gallhills, Kirkpatrick Fleming, Dumfries-shire, died in Jamaica on 22 September 1796. [Kirkconnel gravestone, Dumfries-shire]

SMITH, HUGH, an Anti-Burgher and a shoemaker, was admitted as a burgess and guild-brother of Ayr on 16 August 1815. [ABR]

SMITH, JAMES, in Edingham, Urr, Dumfries-shire, testament, 1794, Comm. Dumfries. [NRS]

SMITH, JAMES, in Selthorns, Middlebie, Dumfries-shire, testament, 1799, Comm. Dumfries. [NRS]

SMITH, JAMES, a sailor in Ayr, testament, 1823, Comm. Glasgow. [NRS]

SMITH, JAMES LEONARD, from Glen Irvine, married Isabella Barker in Guelph, Upper Canada, on 22 October 1844. [AJ.5059]

SMITH, JAMES, born 1811, son of James Smith and his wife Eliabeth Watson, died in the West Indies on 1 April 1853. [Inchinnan gravestone, Renfrewshire]

SMITH, JAMES, in Philadelphia, Pennsylvania, brother and heir of Jean Smith in Kilmarnock, Ayrshire, who died in April 1841. [NRS.S/H]

SMITH, JAMES, born 1833, died in Port au Prince, Haiti, on 22 December 1852. [Caerlaverock gravestone, Dumfries-shire]

SMITH, JAMES, a saddler in Canada, grandson and heir of Andrew Smith an overseer in Orchardton, Kirkcudbrightshire, 1858. [NRS.S/H]

SMITH, JANET, relict of William Irving in Allerbeck, testament, 1793, Comm. Dumfries. [NRS]

SMITH, JOHN, in Cleughside, Glencairn, testament, 1793, Comm. Dumfries. [NRS]

SMITH, JOHN, son of Reverend Samuel Smith, [1757-1816], and his wife Janet Carruthers, [1758-1831], a merchant in New York. [Borgue gravestone, Kirkcudbrightshire]

SMITH, Dr JOHN, born 1796, son of Thomas Smith, [1795-1809], and his wife Agnes Carson, [1757-1811], died on Goshen Estate, Jamaica, in 1826. [Dalry gravestone]

SMITH, Captain JOHN, born 24 August 1824, a shipmaster, drowned in the wreck of the Maju when bound from Dundee to Rangoon, Burma, on 21 October 1874. [Riccarton gravestone, Ayrshire]

SMITH, PETER, from Galloway, a merchant in Halifax, Nova Scotia, for 30 years, died there on 5 May 1816. [AR.11.5.1816]

SMITH, ROBERT, born 14 August 1804, son of James Smith, [1777-1863], a merchant in Greenock, and his wife Ann Farm, [1777-1851], a merchant in Quebec, died on 16 May 1842. [Johnstone gravestone, Renfrewshire]

SMITH, ROBERT, agent in Girvan, Ayrshire, for the Western Bank of Scotland in1849. [POD]

SMITH, THOMAS, minister at Cummertrees, testament, 1800, Comm. Dumfries. [NRS]

SMITH, THOMAS, born 1746 in Edingham, son of James Smith a blacksmith, a minister of the Seceder congregation in Huntington, Pennsylvania, died on 24 August 1825. [Colvend gravestone, Kirkcudbrightshire]

SMITH, WALTER, born 1784 in Ayrshire, died in Georgia on 13 May 1840. [Georgia gravestone]

SMITH, WILLIAM, from Kilmarnock, Ayrshire, a merchant in Charleston, South Carolina, was naturalised there in 1799. [SCA]

SMITH, WILLIAM, born 1796, son of Thomas Smith, [1756-1809], and his wife Agnes Carson, [1757-1811], died on Dunkley Estate, Jamaica, in 1823. [Dalry gravestone]

SMITH, Mrs, born 1798, wife of John Smith from Drongan, Ayrshire, died aboard the Providence in the Bay of Bengal, India, on 30 May 1825. [BM.18.779]

SMYTH, KIRKPATRICK DICKSON, born in Barscar, Dumfries-shire, a student at Edinburgh University, a minister in Bathurst, New South Wales, Australia, from 1835 until 1854, died in Scotland in 1863. [F.7.598]

SNODGRASS, HUGH, son of Hugh Snodgrass a writer in Paisley, Renfrewshire, was educated at Glasgow University around 1784, died in Port Royal, Jamaica, on 24 October 1819. [Car.4.17] [MAGU]

SNODGRASS, JAMES, agent in Stewarton, Ayrshire, for the Western Bank of Scotland in 1849. [POD]

SNODGRASS, NEIL, born 1774, son of Hew Snodgrass, [1747-1807], and his wife Henrietta Somerville, [1747-1798], in Paisley, Renfrewshire, died in Jamaica in 1817. [S.I.48.17] [Paisley gravestone]

SOMERVAIL, WILLIAM, born 1803, a wool-spinner at Haplandmill, died 18 December 1876, husband of Katherine G. Frame, born 1804, died 15 September 1888. [Dunlop gravestone, Ayrshire]

SPEIR, ALEXANDER, in Pishenlinn, Moon Township, Pennsylvania, a deed 18 July 1816. [NRS.RD.Renfrew.6/164]

SPEIRS, ARCHIBALD, versus the Glasgow, Paisley, and Ardrossan Canal Company, 1818. [NRS.CS233.S.10.1]

SPIERS, JAMES, an engineer in San Francisco, California, son and heir of James Spiers in Levernbank, Neilston, Renfrewshire, who died 29 September 1865. [NRS.S/H]

SPIERS, MARGARET BRUCE, daughter of Archibald Spiers of Ellerslie, Renfrewshire, died in Wiesbaden, Germany, on 12 November 1858. [W.XIX.2034]

SPIER, ROBERT, agent of the Union Bank of Scotland in Beith, Ayrshire, in 1849. [POD]

SPENCE, JOHN, from Greenock, settled in America by 1801. [NRS.CS17.1.9/441]

SPOTTISWOODE, ROBERT, son of William Spottiswoode of Glenfernate, [1747-1830], and his wife Janet Mitchell, [1770-1826], died in America in 1855. [Kirkmichael gravestone]

SPROTT, JAMES, died in Stranraer, Wigtownshire, in October 1823, father of Reverend John Sprott and James Sprott in Nova Scotia. [AR.7.2.1824]

SPROTT, JAMES, from Wigtownshire, and Lemoira Smith, daughter of Archibald Smith in Kennetcook, Nova Scotia, were married in Newport, N.S., on 11 April 1822. [AR.27.4.1822]

SPROTT, Reverend JOHN, born March 1790 in Caldons, Stoneykirk, Wigtownshire, educated at Edinburgh University from 1808 until 1812, and at Theological Hall, licensed in 1809, joined the Relief Church and emigrated to Nova Scotia in 1818, a minister in Musquodoboit, N.S., from 1825 until 1845, died on 16 September 1869. [HPC] [RPC]

STAFFORD, MARTIN, a skipper in Greenock, testament, 1826 Comm. Edinburgh. [NRS]

STAIG, CHARLES, third son of David Staig the Provost of Dumfries, died in Tobago in 1795. [SM.57.682]

STEEL, JAMES, a sailor in Saltcoats, Ayrshire, testament, 1807, Comm. Glasgow. [NRS]

STEEL, ROBERT MEGGAT, born in Ayrshire, a shipmaster in New York, married Isabella White on 9 February 1804, was drowned in 1813. [ANY]

STENHOUSE, JOHN, a wright from Greenock, settled in America by 1796. [NRS.CS17.1.15/399]

STEPHENSON, ALEXANDER, born 1805, son of Richard Stevenson and his wife Agnes Armstrong, died in Jamaica on 22 June 1826. [Graitney gravestone, Dumfries-shire]

STEPHENSON, THOMAS, born 1797, son of Richard Stevenson and his wife Agnes Armstrong, died in Jamaica on 3 October 1818. [Graitney gravestone, Dumfries-shire]

STEPHENSON, WILLIAM, born 1795, son of Richard Stevenson and his wife Agnes Armstrong, died in Jamaica on 18 June 1835. [Graitney gravestone, Dumfries-shire]

STEUART, JAMES HOPE, born 20 December 1828 in Gillesbie, son of James Hope Steuart and his wife Helen Bell, died in Port of Spain, Trinidad, on 18 March 1859. [Dryfesdale gravestone, Dumfries-shire]

STEVEN, JAMES, master of the Warner of Saltcoats from Greenock to Savannah, Georgia, in 1817. [NRS.E504.15.116]

STEVEN, Reverend JAMES, born 1801, ordained in Stranraer, Wigtownshire, emigrated to Chaleur, New Brunswick, a minister in N.B. from 1831 until his death on 22 January 1864. [HPC]

STEVENSON, ALEXANDER, agent in Langholm, Dumfries-shire, for the British Linen Company in 1849. [POD]

STEVENSON, ARCHIBALD, born 1758 in Wigtownshire, emigrated to New Brunswick in 1824, was killed by a falling tree at St David, N.B.

STEVENSON, GABRIEL, a merchant in Hamburg, Germany, son and heir of Mary Fleming or Stevenson in Kilmarnock, who died on 27 April 1842. [NRS.S/H]

STEVENSON, ISABELLA, born 1794, daughter of William Clarke late of Shutterflat, Beith, Ayrshire, died at Bankside, Scarboro, Canada West, on 20 May 1848. [SG.1730]

STEVENSON, JOHN, in Netherhill, born 1778, died 23 July 1842, husband of Janet Kerr, born 1804, died in Greenock on 11 May 1875. [Dunlop gravestone, Ayrshire]

STEVENSON, ROBERT, a joiner in Sparta, Randulf County, Illinois, nephew and heir of Matthew Stevenson a feuar in Neilston, Renfrewshire, who died on 16 December 1867. [NRS.S/H]

STEWART, ARCHIBALD, born 1789 in Paisley, Renfrewshire, declared his intention to naturalise in Norfolk Borough Court, Virginia, on 23 February 1829.

STEWART, ARCHIBALD, master of the Cessnock of Irvine from Greenock bound for New York in 1817. [NRS.E504.15.116]

STEWART, GEORGE GORDON, a Commander in the Royal Navy, testament, 1827, Comm. Dumfries. [NRS]

STEWART, JAMES, born 13 November 1785, a merchant in Greenock and in Newfoundland by 1813, died on 11 November 1837. [Greenock gravestone][NRS.SC53.56.I/iii]

STEWART, JAMES, a former partner of J. and J. Stewart merchants in Paisley, a merchant in New York in 1813. [NRS.CS230.S13.1]

STEWART, JAMES, born 1811 in Greenock, Renfrewshire, emigrated to New York in 1830, a builder who died there on 22 September 1876. [ANY]

STEWART, JAMES, a skipper in Greenock, testament, 1822, Comm. Glasgow. [NRS]

STEWART, JAMES, a merchant in Paisley, Renfrewshire, emigrated via Greenock to Bristol, Rhode Island, settled in New York by 1812. [NRS.CS230.Misc.24.1]

STEWART, JAMES, born in Kilmarnock, Ayrshire, settled in Darien, Georgia, in 1818, died at Lower Bluff, Georgia, on 20 August 1822. [Darien Gazette, 4.8.1822]

STEWART, JOHN, born 1802, died in Lucesco, Pennsylvania, on 19 December 1894. [Whithorn gravestone, Galloway]

STEWART, JOHN MCGREGOR, born 1824, died in New Orleans, Louisiana, in February 1858. [Inverkip Street gravestone, Greenock]

STEWART, PETER, a coal hewer at Sourlie, Irvine, Ayrshire, was accused of assault in April 1817. [NRS.JC26.1817.225]

STEWART, ROBERT FARQUHAR SHAW, son of Sir Michael Shaw Stewart of Ardgowan, Renfrewshire, married Isabella Jane Warner, eldest daughter of Charles W. Warner, HM Attorney General of Trinidad, in Port of Spain, Trinidad, on 10 February 1859. [EEC.3345] [CM.21689]

STEWART, ROGER, born 1822, died in Springhill, Mobile, Alabama, on 25 May 1858. [Inverkip Street gravestone, Greenock]

STEWART, WILLIAM, a shoemaker in 22 St Mirren Street, Paisley, with five sons and two daughters, applied to settle in Canada on 7 May 1819. [TNA.CO384.5.871]

STEWART, SHANNON, & Co., merchants in Greenock and Newfoundland, sederunt book, 1816-1830. [NRS.CS96.905.1-6]

STIRLING, WILLIAM, an innkeeper, was admitted as a burgess and freeman of Ayr on 10 September 1800. [ABR]

STIRRAT, DAVID, in Baltimore, Maryland, cousin and heir of Elizabeth Gavin in Beith, Ayrshire, 1834. [NRS.S/H]

STIRRAT, DAVID, in Monhaven, North America, son and heir of David Stirrat, a sewen muslin manufacturer in Kilwinning, Ayrshire, who died on 27 October 1859. [NRS.S/H]

STOBO, JOHN, master of the <u>Frances Anne of Irvine</u> from Fort William bound for Pictou, Nova Scotia, in 1817. [NRS.E504.12.6]

STOREY, Dr WILLIAM, from Dumfries, died in the West Indies in 1818. [S.2.85.18]

STORMONTH-DARLING, JAMES, agent in Kelso, Roxburghshire, for the Bank of Scotland in 1849. [POD]

STOTHART, JAMES, born 1774, son of Andrew Stothart and his wife Mary Little in Gretna, Dumfries-shire, settled at Montego Bay, St James, Jamaica, died on 6 February 1818. [Montego Bay gravestone] [Graitney gravestone, Dumfries-shire]

STOTHART, THOMAS, of Arkland, a writer in Dumfries, testament, 1792, Comm. Dumfries. [NRS]

STOTHART, THOMAS, born 1825, eldest son of John Stothart in Crossbankhead, Dumfries-shire, died in Priceville, County Gray, Canada West, on17 April 1885. [S.13065]

STOTT, JAMES, at Newbridge of Clouden, Terregles, testament, 1794, Comm. Dumfries. [NRS]

STRATHEARN, JOHN, a journeyman wright from Kilmarnock, now in Glasgow, versus his wife Flora MacDougal, a servant in Broomhill, Lanark, a Process of Divorce in 1801. [NRS.CC8.6.1108]

STREHORN, JOHN, formerly a farmer in Clydeneuck, Ayrshire, now in America by 1820. [NRS.CS17.1.39/490]

STRUTHERS, GEORGE, son of John Struthers a farmer in Sorn, Ayrshire, was educated at Glasgow University in 1807, a minister in Cornwallis, Nova Scotia, from 1822 until his death there on 19 March 1857. [MAGU]

SUTHERLAND, ALEXANDER, from St Vincent, married Magdalene Webster, daughter of John Webster in Gourock, Renfrewshire, there on 7 July 1800. [GC.1386]

SWAN, JAMES, from Ayrshire, a mason in Halifax, Nova Scotia, probate, 1842, Halifax, N.S.

SWAN, JOHN, formerly in Cocketfield, later in Searigg, Dalton, testament, 1793, Comm. Dumfries. [NRS]

TAIT, ANDREW, in Barhead of Edingham, Urr, testament, 1794, Comm. Dumfries. [NRS]

TAIT, JAMES, a land surveyor in Lockerbie, testament, 1797, Comm. Dumfries. [NRS]

TAIT, JOHN, in Holestaine, testament, 1798, Comm. Dumfries. [NRS]

TAIT, JOHN, born 1809 in Moffat, Dumfries-shire, son of William Tat and his wife Catherine Beattie, was educated at Glasgow University in 1833, emigrated to Australia in 1837, a minister in New South Wales and in Victoria from 1837 until his death on 19 March 1860. [F.7.599]

TAIT, or GIBSON, MARGARET, in Rockford, Illinois, daughter and heir of John Tait in Cartyloop, Minnigaff, Kirkcudbrightshire, 1838. [NRS.S/H]

TAIT, PETER, born 1792, died in Tobago on 8 July 1859. [Balmaclellan gravestone, Kirkcudbrightshire]

TAIT, WILLIAM, born 1809, son of James Tait in Newton, Stewart, Dumfries-shire, a surgeon who died in Quebec on 14 June 1831. [FH.543]

TASKER, PATRICK, born 1823 in Greenock, Renfrewshire, settled in St John's, Newfoundland, as an employee of Hunter and Company. [MU.mf313]

TASSIE, ELIZABETH, born 1784, nurse to the family of Wallace of Lochryan, died 6 May 1880. [Cairnryan gravestone, Wigtownshire]

TASSIE, JAMES, agent of the Western Bank of Scotland in Eaglesham, Renfrewshire, in 1849. [POD]

TAYLOR, ELIZABETH, born 1775, daughter of Robert Taylor, [1770-1831], a merchant, and his wife Jean Taylor, [1770-1846], wife of James Melville, died in Wetheredville, USA, on 20 October 1866. [Barrhead gravestone, Renfrewshire]

TAYLOR, JAMES, born 1799, son of Robert Taylor, [1770-1831], a merchant, and his wife Jean Taylor, [1770-1846], wife of James Melville, a civil engineer in Trinidad, died on 26 January 1824. [Arthurlie, Barrhead gravestone, Renfrewshire]

TAYLOR, JANETTE, born 1776 in Dumfries, a niece of John Paul Jones, emigrated to America in 1828, died in New York on 5 March 1844. [EEC.20013] [AJ.5021]

TAYLOR, ROBERT, from Jamaica, married Jane Burnside, daughter of the minister of St Michael's, Dumfries, there in 1813. [EA.5218.13]

TAYLOR, ..., from Irvine, Ayrshire, settled on Cape Breton, Nova Scotia, before 1819, brother of Henry Talor. [NRS.CS38.1819]

TEDCASTLE, JOHN, in Centre Hill, Hudson City, North America, son and heir of Janet Hope or Tedcastle, wife of Thomas Walker in Maxwelltown, Dumfries-shire, 1864. [NRS.S/H]

TELFAIR, EDWARD, born 1735 in the Stewartry of Kirkcudbright, emigrated to America in 1758, settled in Virginia, North Carolina, and Georgia, a merchant and politician, died in Savannah, Georgia, in 1807. [TSA]

TELFER, ELIZABETH, widow of ... Reid a saddler in Ayr, died in Montreal, Quebec, on 11 August 1832. [AJ.4422]

TELFER, JAMES, a merchant, was admitted as a burgess and guilds-brother of Ayr on 24 September 1800. [ABR]

TELFER, JAMES, born 1796 in Dumfries-shire, son of Robert Telfer, emigrated to Canada in 1821, settled in Caverhill, Queensbury, New Brunswick. [PANB]

TELFER, JOHN, in Wester Kirkhope, testament, 1797, Comm. Dumfries. [NRS]

TELFER, JOHN, born 1799 in Dumfries-shire, son of Robert Telfer, emigrated to Canada in 1821, settled in Caverhill, Queensbury, New Brunswick. [PANB]

TELFER, ROBERT, born 1771 in Dumfres-shire, a carpenter and farmer, with family, emigrated to Canada in 1821, was granted land in Caverhill, New Brunswick. [PANB]

TELFORD, THOMAS, born 1757 in Glendining, Westerkirk parish, Dumfries-shire, bridgebuilder and civil engineer, died in London on 2 September 1834. [Westminster Abbey MI]

TEMPLETON, GILBERT, born 1825, a shepherd from Ayrshire, landed in Hobart, Tasmania, Australia, from the White Star in 1855. [SRA.TD292]

TEMPLETON, WILLIAM, in Braehead, born 1788, died 4 January 1871, husband of Janet Andrew, born 1788, died 20 February 1874. [Riccarton gravestone, Ayrshire]

THOM, CHARLES, in Plainfield, New Jersey, grandson and heir of Charles Thom in Paisley, Renfrewshire, who died 10 June 1845. [NRS.S/H]

THOM, JOHN ALFRED, a clerk in Brazil, grandson of William Ferguson, a coal merchant in Greenock, who died on 24 March 1841. [NRS.S/H]

THOMSON, ADAM, born 1 October 1820 in Paisley, died at Prospect Hill, Montego Bay, St James, Jamaica, on 9 December 1897. [Montego Bay gravestone]

THOMPSON, ARCHIBALD, emigrated from Dumfries-shire to Canada in 1800. [SO]

THOMSON, A., cashier of the Greenock Bank in 1849. [POD]

THOMPSON, D., master of the Merlin of Greenock from Greenock with passengers bound for Quebec in 1847. [BPP]

THOMSON, DAVID, born 1764, a stonemason in Wester Kirk, Dumfries-shire, emigrated with Mary Glendinning and their four children to Canada in 1795. [SO]

THOMPSON, DOUGALD, a farmer in Birchville, North America, grandson and heir of Donald Thompson a farmer in Greenock, Renfrewshire, who died 22 January 1839. [NRS.S/H]

THOMPSON, JAMES, born 1779 in Lockerbie, Dumfries-shire, emigrated to New Brunswick in 1816, a minister in Newcastle and in Chatham on the Miramachi River, N.B., from 1817 until his death on 11 November 1830. [HPC]

THOMSON, Captain JAMES, in Dumfries, testaments, 1798/1799, Comm. Dumfries. [NRS]

THOMSON, JAMES, born 1780, son of Joh Thomson a manufacturer in Wamphrae, Dumfries-shire, was educated at Glasgow University in 1797, minister at Auchtergaven, Perthshire, from 1806 until 1816, then minister at Miramachi, New Brunswick, from 1816 until his death on 11 October 1830. [MAGU]

THOMSON, JOHN, born 1742, son of William Thomson and his wife Agnes Aitken, died in North Carolina in July 1796. [Colvend gravestone, Kirkcudbrightshire]

THOMSON, JOHN, a farmer from Glenin, Sanquhar, Dumfries-shire, died at Wentworth Castle, St Mary's, Jamaica, on 31 May 1802. [EA.4050.02]

THOMPSON, JOHN, born 1777, formerly a merchant in Dumfries, settled in St John, New Brunswick, died at Morris Street, St John, on 26 January 1840. [MCN.29.1.1840]

THOMSON, PETER, born 1770, son of Robert Thomson, [1717-1783], and his wife Agnes Lewers, [1741-1811], died in Philadelphia, Pennsylvania, on 16 July 1795. [Colvend gravestone, Kirkcudbrightshire]

THOMSON, ROBERT, in Barhead, Orchardton, Kirkcudbrightshire, a victim of theft in 1824. [NRS.AD14.24.150]

THOMSON, ROBERT, born 1817, son of James Thomson, a missionary in Tahiti, died on 1 January 1854. [St Michael's gravestone, Dumfries]

THOMSON, ROBERT, messenger at arms, Beith, Ayrshire, 1849. [POD]

THOMSON, THOMAS, born 1791, late in Jamaica, died in August 1849. [Whithorn gravestone, Wigtownshire]

THOMSON, WILLIAM, MD, son of John Thomson a writer in Kirkcudbright, died in Richmond, St Mary's, Jamaica, in 1802. [AJ.2677]

THOMSON, WILLIAM GREGORY, born 1825 in Kilmarnock, Ayrshire, son of Robert Thomson and his wife Mary Gregory, a carpet agent in New York, died in Kilmarnock on17 February 1900. [ANY]

THOMSON, Captain, and Susan Thomson, both from Dumfries, were married in Halifax, Nova Scotia, on 28 June 1818. [FP.30.6.1818]

THOMSON, ..., master of the William and John of Dumfries trading with Ulverston in 1826. [NRS.E504.9.10]

THORBURN, JOHN, son of John Thorburn a farmer in Langholm, Dumfries-shire, a writer in Langholm, was admitted as a Notary Public on 18 June 1799. [NRS.SC62.44.7.439; NP2.36.269]

THRESHIE, ROBERT, agent of the Bank of Scotland in Dumfries in 1849. [POD]

TIVENDALE, THOMAS, a draper, was admitted as a burgess and freeman of Ayr on 8 April 1846. [ABR]

TODD, ALEXANDER, son of Alexander Todd, [1774-1851], and his wife Martha Spiers, [1776-1846], settled in New Orleans, Louisiana. [Houston gravestone, Renfrewshire]

TODD, JOHN, a travelling salesman in Mauchline, Ayrshire, was accused of the culpable homicide of George Halliday in Lockerbie, Dumfries-shire, in 1825. [NRS.AD14.25.43]

TORBET, JOHN, a surgeon in Paisley, Renfrewshire, married Agnes Case Douglas, daughter of Colin Douglas in Demerara, in St Ann's, Limehouse, London, on 21 July 1828. [S.893.490]

TORBET, ROBERT, in Melbourne, Victoria, Australia, brother of John Torbet, a surgeon in Paisley, 1854. [NRS.S/H]

TUDHOPE, ARCHIBALD, born 1801, eldest son of Thomas Tudhope a merchant in Paisley, matriculated at Glasgow University in 1813, minister in Annan from 1834 to 1838, then in Philadelphia, Pennsylvania, and in elsewhere in the USA, died in Cincinnati, Ohio, on 6 September 1861. [RGG]

TURIFF, WILLIAM, born 1828, an overseer, died at Beoch on 23 June 1873. [Cairnryan gravestone, Wigtownshire]

TURNBULL, Dr ANDREW, born 1719 in Annan, Dumfries-shire, a physician in Charleston, South Carolina, died there on 13 May 1792. [SM.54.309]

TURNBULL, ROBERT, a baker in Eaglesham, Renfrewshire, a trial, 1847. [NRS.JC13.91]

TURNER, ARCHIBALD, born 1777 in Greenock, Renfrewshire, died in Aylesford, Nova Scotia, on 1 December 1817. [AR.13.12.1817]

TURNER, THOMAS, agent in Greenock, for the Royal Bank of Scotland in 1849. [POD]

TWADDELL, ROBERT, eldest son of Thomas Twaddell a merchant in Dumfries, settled in America by 1799. [NRS.CS17.1.18/120]

TWEEDIE, JAMES, born 27 August 1797 in Torthorwald, Dumfries-shire, a shoemaker, with his wife Margaret Byars, [1799-1862], and son Thomas Tweedie, born 13 September 1820, emigrated to Canada in 1821, settled in Caverhill, Queensbury, York County, New Brunswick, died on 14 March 1860, buried in Wicklow, N.B. [PANB]

TYRIE, JAMES, born 1758 in Greenock, a shipmaster in New York, later a ships chandler there from 1801 until his death on 16 December 1806. [ANY]

UNDERWOOD, WILLIAM, born 1802, a servant at Gateside, Dumfries-shire, was accused of rape and assault of Agnes Lockerbie in Gilhall, Dumfries-shire, in 1829. [NRS.AD14.29.211]

URIE, JAMES, agent in Kilmarnock, Ayrshire, for the Western Bank of Scotland in 1849. [POD]

VEITCH, JAMES, jr., agent in Sanquhar, Dumfries-shire, for the Western Bank of Scotland in 1849. [POD]

WADDELL, PETER, son of William Waddell, [1712-1781], a mason, and his wife Jean Buttar, died in Jamaica aged 29. [Dumfries gravestone]

WALKER, MATTHEW, from Renfrew, in America by 1809. [NRS.CS17.1.28/320]

WALL, PHILIP, son of Robert Wall, [1781-1846], died in Jamaica aged 33. [Dumfries gravestone]

WALL, WILLIAM HENRY, son of Robert Wall, [1781-1846], died in Port Morant, Jamaica, aged 25. [Dumfries gravestone]

WALLACE, ALEXANDER, from Galston, Ayrshire, died in Moulton, Lake Erie, Niagara District, Canada West, on 8 October 1846. [W.VII.39]

WALLACE, HUGH, from Greenock, a planter and merchant in Biscany, Jamaica, in 1820s. [NRS.CS239.W36.1]

WALLACE, JAMES, minister at Keir, testament, 1800, Comm. Dumfries. [NRS]

WALLACE, JAMES, a sailor in Kirkcolm, inventory, 1822, Comm. Dumfries. [NRS]

WALLACE, JAMES, a victim of assault etc. at the Old Foundry, West Hawkhill farm, St Quivox, Ayrshire, in 1843. [NRS.AD14.43.375]

WALLACE, JAMES, a lithographer in West Saint Louis, USA, heir to his great grandfather William McHoull, a papermaker in Galston, Ayrshire, who died on 5 November 1848. [NRS.S/H]

WALLACE, JOHN, in Mortonholm, parish of Closeburn, testament, 1791, Comm. Dumfries. [NRS]

WALLACE, ROBERT, agent in Langholm, Dumfries-shire, for the National Bank of Scotland in 1849. [POD]

WALLACE, ROBERT, a messenger at arms in Dumfries in 1849. [POD]

WALKER, ARCHIBALD, son of Robert Walker, [1735-1805], and his wife Herries Gray, died in Virginia on 5 February 1805. [Dumfries gravestone]

WALLACE, JOHN, surgeon in Waterside of Fenwick, Ayrshire, accused of procuring an abortion by drugs in 1842. [NRS.AC14.42.95]

WALTERS, Captain, master of the Hound of Greenock from Greenock bound for St John's, New Brunswick, in 1844 and 1849. [GSP]

WARNOCK, JOHN, in Australia, son of Andrew Warnock, a manufacturer in Paisley, who died on 28 May 1853. [NRS.S/H]

WARWICK, MATILDA, daughter of Peter Warwick in Kirkcudbright, married Peter Stubs cashier of the Charlotte County Bank, in St Andrews, New Brunswick, on 12 December 1831. [NBC.17.12.131]

WATLING, THOMAS, a painter in Dumfries, found guilty at Dumfries of forging bank notes on 15 April 1789, was sentenced to be transported to the colonies for fourteen years, [AJ.2154]

WATSON, HUGH, born 1778 in the parish of Mearns, Renfrewshire, a carpet weaver, husband of Elizabeth who was born in Kilwinning, Ayrshire, with children Robert, Janet, Matthew, George, and William, all born in Paisley between 1805 and 1811, emigrated via Greenock to USA, were naturalised in New York on 18 March 1822. [NARA]

WATSON, JAMES, born 1812 in Eaglesham, Renfrewshire, died in Paterson, New Jersey, on 16 August 1873. [GH.10509]

WATSON, JAMES, born 11 February 1799 in Johnstone, Renfrewshire, a divinity student in 1823, later a pastor and missionary in Kingston, Jamaica, from 1827 until 1868, died in Edinburgh on 17 May 1873. [AUPC] [St Andrew's Presbyterian Church plaque] [Lucea gravestone, Hanover, Jamaica]

WATSON, JOHN, from Greenock, Renfrewshire, died in Wilmington, North Carolina, in January 1804. [SM.66.320]

WATSON, WILLIAM, master of the Janet of Irvine from Greenock to Halifax, Nova Scotia, in 1814. [NRS.E504.15.105]

WAUGH, ADAM, agent in Lochmaben, Dumfries-shire, for the National Bank of Scotland in 1849. [POD]

WEAL, ANDREW, born 1776, former baron officer to the Duke of Buccleugh at Langholm, Dumfries-shire, died in Flambro West, Canada West, on 2 July 1846. [W.VII.721]

WEBSTER, MAGDALENE, daughter of John Webster in Gourock, Renfrewshire, married Alexander Sutherland from St Vincent, in Gourock on 7 July 1800. [GC.1386]

WEIR, ALEXANDER, a bookseller from Paisley, a bookseller in New York, husband of Sarah Collins, probate 26 October 1790, N.Y.

WEIR, JAMES, a merchant in Dumfries, testament, 1795, Comm. Dumfries. [NRS]

WEIR, ROBERT, born 1770 in Paisley, Renfrewshire, son of Walter Weir a merchant, settled in New York as a skipper and merchant, died there on 5 February 1825. [ANY]

WELLS, JOHN, born 1832 son of Robert Wells in Dumfries-shire, was educated at Glasgow University around 1856, later a minister in New Brunswick from 1861. [F.7.612]

WEMYSS, WILLIAM, a butcher and spirit dealer in Dumfries, was accused of sheep stealing in 1846. [NRS.AD14.46.301]

WHITE, ALEXANDER, born 1778, son of John White at Bladnoch Bridge, Wigtownshire, died in Mobile, Alabama, on 2 March 1823. [Wigtown gravestone]

WHITE, GEORGE, from Dumfries, and Margaret, the widow of Captain Cook in Lunenburg, Nova Scotia, were married in Londonderry, N.S., on 1 October 1829. [AR.10.10.1829]

WHITE, JAMES, agent in Muirkirk for the Western Bank of Scotland in 1849. [POD]

WHITE, WILLIAM, a mariner in Kirkcudbright, testament, 1819, Comm. Kirkcudbright. [NRS]

WHITEHEAD, Captain, master of the Neirid of Dumfries from Dumfries to America in1830. [QM.28.4.1830]

WHITEWRIGHT, WILLIAM, born 8 July 1783 in Balmaghie, Kirkcudbrightshire, settled in New York by 1831, died there on 8 May 1874. [ANY]

WHYTE, JOHN, shipmaster of the sloop Hope of Greenock testament, 28 April 1798, Comm. Argyll. [NRS]

WILKIE, JAMES, Captain of the brig Swinger of Greenock, testament, 1802, Comm. Glasgow. [NRS]

WILKIN, WILLIAM, born 1789, son of James Wilkin a farmer in North Kirkblain, and his wife Helen McMorine, died in Jamaica on 22 June 1827. [Caerlaverock gravestone, Dumfries-shire]

WILLIAMS, JAMES, born in Kirkcudbright, agent for Lord Selkirk, emigrated to Prince Edward Island on the Oughton in 1803, possibly settled in Louisiana in 1815. [DCB]

WILLIAMSON, ANDREW, an Anti-Burgher, was admitted as a burgess and guild-brother of Ayr on 12 September 1804. [ABR]

WILLIAMSON, JAMES, son of John Williamson a writer in Annan, and his wife Dorothea Wallace, settled in St Anne's, Jamaica, died 1793. [Annan gravestone, Dumfries-shire]

WILLIAMSON, JAMES, of Riddings, testament, 1795, Comm. Dumfries. [NRS]

WILLIAMSON, JOHN, a ropemaker in Dumfries, testament, 1800, Comm. Dumfries. [NRS]

WILLIAMSON, JOHN, a merchant, emigrated via Greenock aboard the brig Portaferry bound for Quebec in 1833. [MG.30.5.1833]

WILLIAMSON, THOMAS, a writer in Dumfries, deceased, father of Susan and David Williamson in Edinburgh, a deed, 1825. [NRS.GD19.278]

WILLIAMSON, WILLIAM, born 22 July 1849 in Kirkmaiden-in-Rhinns, Wigtownshire, son of Reverend William Williamson and his wife Mary McDowall, settled in Detroit, Michigan. [F.2.342]

WILLIS, THOMAS, MD, from Annandale, Dumfries-shire, died in Annandale, St Ann's, Jamaica, on 6 September 1841. [AJ.4898] [EEC20284]

WILSON, DAVID, master of the Ocean of Ayr from Ayr to Quebec in 1806; master of the Caledonia of Ayr from Ayr to Quebec in 1806. [NRS.E504.4.11]

WILSON, ANDREW, messenger at arms, Kilmarnock, 1849. [POD]

WILSON, JAMES, farmer in Dangton, born 1785, died 4 December 1864, husband of Grace Robertson, born 1796, died 19 January 1841. [Dunlop gravestone, Ayrshire]

WILSON, JOHN, of Bogrie, a merchant in Dumfries, testament, 1799, Comm. Dumfries. [NRS]

WILSON, JOHN, in Paisley, Renfrewshire, applied to settle in Canada on 2 March 1815. [NRS.RH9]

WILSON, JOHN R., born 1773 in Saltcoats, Ayrshire, of the brig Reliance died in the Marine Hospital, St John, New Brunswick, on 26 August 1842. [St Andrews Standard.2.9.1842]

WILSON, THOMAS, a packman in Maxwelltown, Troquier, Stewartry of Kirkcudbright, was accused of housebreaking, theft, and reset at Hall of Drumpark, Irongray, Kirkcudbrightshire, in 1832. [NRS.AD14.32.57]

WILSON, WILLIAM, a merchant, eldest son of Andrew Wilson the deacon of the Hammermen of Kirkcudbright, died in Antigua on 13 October 1823. [DPCA.1117]

WITHER, DAVID, master of the Mary and June of Stranraer from Greenock to Newfoundland in 1817. [NRS.E504.15.117]

WOODS, JAMES, a merchant in America, later in Ayr by 1787. [NRS.CS17.1.6/334]

WOOD, JANET, former servant of Reverend James Richmond in Irvine, Ayrshire, testament, 1793, Comm. Glasgow. [NRS]

WOOD, JOHN, a bookseller from Dumfries, died in Jamaica on 27 January 1821. [BM.9.363]

WOOD, JOHN, from Netherwood, Dumfries-shire, died in Richmond, Virginia, on 25 December 1822. [SM.90.269]

WOODS, MARGARET, wife of Laurence Kidd, from Kilmarnock, Ayrshire, died in Canada on 23 July 1832. [AJ.4422]

WOODHOUSE, ROBERT, from Dalbeith, a merchant in Savanna, died in 1800, probate 10 July 1800, Chatham County, Georgia.

WOTHERSPOON, JOHN, a Writer to the Signet in Australia, brother and heir of Agnes Wotherspoon in Borgue, Kirkcudbrightshire, 1857. [NRS.S/H]

WOTHERSPOON, OSWALD, in Sydney, New South Wales, Australia, brother and heir of Agnes Wotherspoon in Borgue, Kirkcudbrightshire, 1857. [NRS.S/H]

WRIGHT. JAMES, born 1807, son of George Wright a writer in Lockerbie, Dumfries-shire, died in Tobago on 14 May 1832. [Dryfesdale gravestone, Dumfries-shire]

WRIGHT, JAMES, from Bridge of Weir, Renfrewshire, bound via Quebec to settle in Upper Canada in 1820. [NRS.SC58.75.79]

WRIGHT, JOHN, a hawker, accused of theft, failed to appear at his trial, so was outlawed in Ayr in 1820. [NRS.JC26.1820.129]

WRIGHT, JAMES, in Newton Stewart, Wigtownshire, emigrated via Sligo, Ireland, to New York aboard the Juno on 16 August 1816. [NWI]

WRIGHT, JAMES, born 1774 in Riccarton, died in Muirkirk on 27 November 1839; his brother William Wright, born 1764, died 15 November 1844. [Riccarton gravestone, Ayrshire]

WRIGHT, JAMES, a seaman from Paisley, Renfrewshire, later in America, died April 1859, an inventory, 1860, Edinburgh. [NRS] [Dunlop gravestone, Ayrshire]

WYLIE, ALEXANDER, in Hazelbank, born 1762, died 20 March 1840, husband of Janet Creighton, born 1766, died 11 April 1847, parents of Marion Wylie, born 1805, died 2 May 1826, and Robert Wylie, MD, a merchant in Mazathon, Mexico.

WYLIE, ALEXANDER, in East Halket, born 1792, died 25 March 1869, husband of Jane Foulds, born 1805, died 19 October 1855. [Dunlop gravestone, Ayrshire]

WYLIE, HUGH, a merchant in Kilmarnock, Ayrshire, testament, 1796, Comm. Glasgow. [NRS]

WYLIE, J., in Ayr, applied to settle in Canada on 4 March 1815. [NRS.RH9]

WYLIE, JAMES, a skipper in Greenock, testament, 1814, Comm. Glasgow. [NRS]

WYLIE, JOHN, in Leehouses, testament, 1794, Comm. Dumfries. [NRS]

WYLIE, JOHN, master of the Kelly of Greenock, testament, 1812, Comm. Edinburgh. [NRS]

WYLIE, JOHN, in Halket, born 1755, died 12 February 1837, husband of Margaret ...., born 1757, died25 October 1836. [Dunlop gravestone, Ayrshire]

WYLLIE, JOHN, a glover in Orleans, Vermont, a sasine, 15 November 1864. [NRS.Whithorn,4/35.43]

WYLIE, ROBERT C., son of Alexander Wylie, [1762-1840], and his wife Janet Creighton, [1766-1847], a physician and merchant in Mexico. [Dunlop gravestone, Ayrshire]

WYLIE, ..., master of the Tryall of Annan trading between Ulverston and Dumfries in 1825. [NRS.E504.9.10]

WYLIE, Captain, master of the Favourite of Greenock from Greenock bound for Quebec in 1848. [MG]

WYPER, DAVID, born 1805, a clogger in Lockerbie, Dumfries-shire, was accused of assaulting and robbing Jean Dobie in High Street, Lockerbie, in 1830. [NRS.AD14.30.146]

YOUNG, AGNES, spouse of John Fulton a farmer in Eaglesham, Renfrewshire, testament, 1795, Comm. Glasgow. [NRS]

YOUNG, ALEXANDER, born 1773, Speaker of the House of Assembly in New Providence in the Bahamas, died in Nassau on 6 September 1813. [Dumfries gravestone]

YOUNG, ANDREW, sr., at Holmhead, testament, 1794, Comm. Glasgow. [NRS]

YOUNG, ANDREW, in Upper Canada, nephew and heir of John Richmond in Houletburn, Loudon Castle, Ayrshire, 1848. [NRS.S/H]

YOUNG, ANDREW HOUSTON, from Quebec, married Janet Greenshields, second daughter of Thomas Greenshields, in Kilmarnock, Ayrshire, on 12 January 1841. [GM.ns.15.200]

YOUNG, GEORGE, a carpet manufacturer in Kilmarnock, Ayrshire, testament, 1790, Comm. Glasgow. [NRS]

YOUNG, GEORGE, born 1800, a manufacturer in Kilmarnock, Ayrshire, died 5 January 1854, husband of Mary Bain, born 1802, died 27 June 1855. [Riccarton gravestone, Ayrshire]

YOUNG, HUGH, a stonecutter in New York, son and heir of James Young a mason in Kilmarnock, Ayrshire, who died on 26 April 1860. [NRS.S/H]

YOUNG, JAMES, in Ayr, applied to settle in Canada on 4 March 1815. [NRS.RH9]

YOUNG, JAMES, born 1823 in New York, a seaman resident in Taylor's Close, Greenock, accused of assault in 1850. [NRS.AD14.50.40]

YOUNG, JOHN, a mariner in Maryport, Dumfries-shire, a testament, 1823, Comm. Dumfries. [NRS]

YOUNG, JOHN, in Ayr, applied to settle in Canada on 4 March 1815. [NRS.RH9]

YOUNG JOHN, born 1811 in Ayr, emigrated to Canada in 1826, a merchant and politician there. [BCB]

YOUNG, JOHN, son of James Young, a merchant in Galston, Ayrshire, and his wife Margaret Mason, [1784-1811], settled in Hamilton, Canada. [Loudoun gravestone, Ayrshire]

YOUNG, JOHN, a cooper in Griffen Town, Montreal, Quebec, heir to his uncle John Young, a farmer in Blackston, later in Bishoptown, Renfrewshire, who died on 28 January 1843. [NRS.S/H]

YOUNG, MARY, wife of Joseph Millar in St John, New Brunswick, son and heir of Isabella Cowden, widow of William Millar a carter in Glencaple, Dumfriesshire, 1869. [NRS.S/H]

YOUNG, THOMAS, born 1845, died in Joplin, Missouri, on 5 September 1873. [Dunlop gravestone, Ayrshire]

YOUNG, WILLIAM, of Rig of Graitney, [Gretna], testament,1796, Comm. Dumfries. [NRS]

YULE, ARCHIBALD, late of the Dumfries Militia, applied to settle in Canada on 2 May 1827. [TNA.CO384.16.1E]

REFERENCES

AA Ayr Archives

ABR Ayr Burgess Roll

AJ Aberdeen Journal, series

ANY St Andrews Society of New York

AO Annan Observer, series

AP St Andrews Society of Philadelphia

AR Acadian Review, series

ARM Madeira Regional Archives, Funchal

AUPC Annals of the United Presbyterian Church, [Edinburgh

BA Officers of the Bengal Army, 1758-1834, [London, 1927-1946]

BCB Biographies of Celebrated Canadians, [Quebec, 1862]

BM Blackwood's Magazine, series

BPP British Parliamentary Papers, series

BSL Boston Shipping Links, series

Car. Caribeanna, series

CG City Gazette, series

CM Caledonian Mercury, series

CMF History of the Clan MacFarlane

CMSA Colonial Museum and Savanna Advertiser, series

CP Canada and its Provinces, [Toronto, 1914]

DCB Dictionary of Canadian Biography

DGA Dumfries and Galloway Archives

DGC Dumfries & Galloway Courier, series

DGH Dumfries and Galloway Herald, series

DCr Dumfries Courier, series

DPCA Dundee, Perth, & Cupar Advertiser, series

DWJ Dumfries Weekly Journal, series

EC Edinburgh Courant, series

EEC Edinburgh Evening Courant, series

EFR   East Fife Record, series

ERA   Edinburgh Register of Apprentices, 1756-1800.[Edinburgh, 1963]

EUL   Edinburgh University Library

EWJ   Edinburgh Weekly Journal series

F   Fasti Ecclesiae Scoticanae, series

FP   Free Press, Halifax, Nova Scotia, series

GA   Greenock Advertiser, series

GBR   Glasgow Burgess Roll

GC   Gordons of Craichlaw, [Dalbeattie, 1924]

GCA   Glasgow City Archives

GH   Glasgow Herald, series

GM   Gentleman's Magazine, series

GNS   Gleaner & Northumberland Schediasma, series

GSP   Glasgow Saturday Post, series

GT   Greenock Telegraph, series

HBRS   Hudson Bay Record Society, Winnipeg

HCA   History of the County of Ayr, [Ayr, 1852]

HGM   Historic Graves of Maryland and the D.C., 1908

HJ   Halifax, Journal, series

HOJ   History of the Johnstones, Edinburgh

HPC   History of the Presbyterian Church, 1885

HT   Halifax Times, series

Imm.NE   Immigrants to New England, [Baltimore, Maryland]

JRG   Jamaica Royal Gazette, series

L Lloyd's

LAC Libraries and Archives, Canada

MAGU Matriculation Album, Glasgow University, [Glasgow, 1913]

MG Montreal Gazette, series

MHS Maritime History of Scotland, [East Linton, 2002]

NARA National Archives, Record Administration, Washington

NBC New Brunswick Courier, series

NBRG New Brunswick Royal Gazette, series

NEHGS New England, Historic Genealogical Society, Boston

NLS National Library of Scotland, Edinburgh

NRS National Records of Scotland, Edinburgh

NYPL New York Public Library

OD Scots in the Old Dominion, [Edinburgh, 1980]

PANB Public Archives of New Brunswick

PCC Prerogative Court of Canterbury

PI Passengers from Ireland, [Baltimore, Maryland, 1980]

POD Post Office Directory, 1849-1850, [Edinburgh, 1849]

QCG Quebec City Gazette, series

QM Quebec Mercury, series

RAF Robertson's Ayrshire Families, [Irvine, 1825]

RCF Records of Clan Ferguson, [Edinburgh. 1899]

RGG Register of Glasgow Graduates

RGNA Royal Gazette & Newfoundland Advertiser, series

RPC Reformed Presbyterian Church in Scotland, [Edinburgh 1925]

RRW   Raleigh Register Weekly, N.C., series

RSC Records of the Scottish Colleges, [Aberdeen, 1913]

S   Scotsman, series

SG   Scottish Guardian, series

SGen   Scottish Genealogist, series

SGS   Scottish Genealogy Society, Edinburgh

SIG   Scots in Germany, [Edinburgh, 1902]

SM   Scots Magazine, series

SO   The Scots Overseas, [London, 1966]

SRA   Strathclyde Regional Archives, Glasgow

TNA   The National Archives, Kew, London

TSA   The Scots in America, [New York, 1896]

UNC   University of North Carolina

UPC   History of the United Presbyterian Church

VSA   Virginia State Archives

W   Witness, series

WO   Weekly Observer, series

www.ingramcontent.com/pod-product-compliance
Lightning Source LLC
Chambersburg PA
CBHW071847230426
43671CB00012B/2093